LIGHT SENSIT

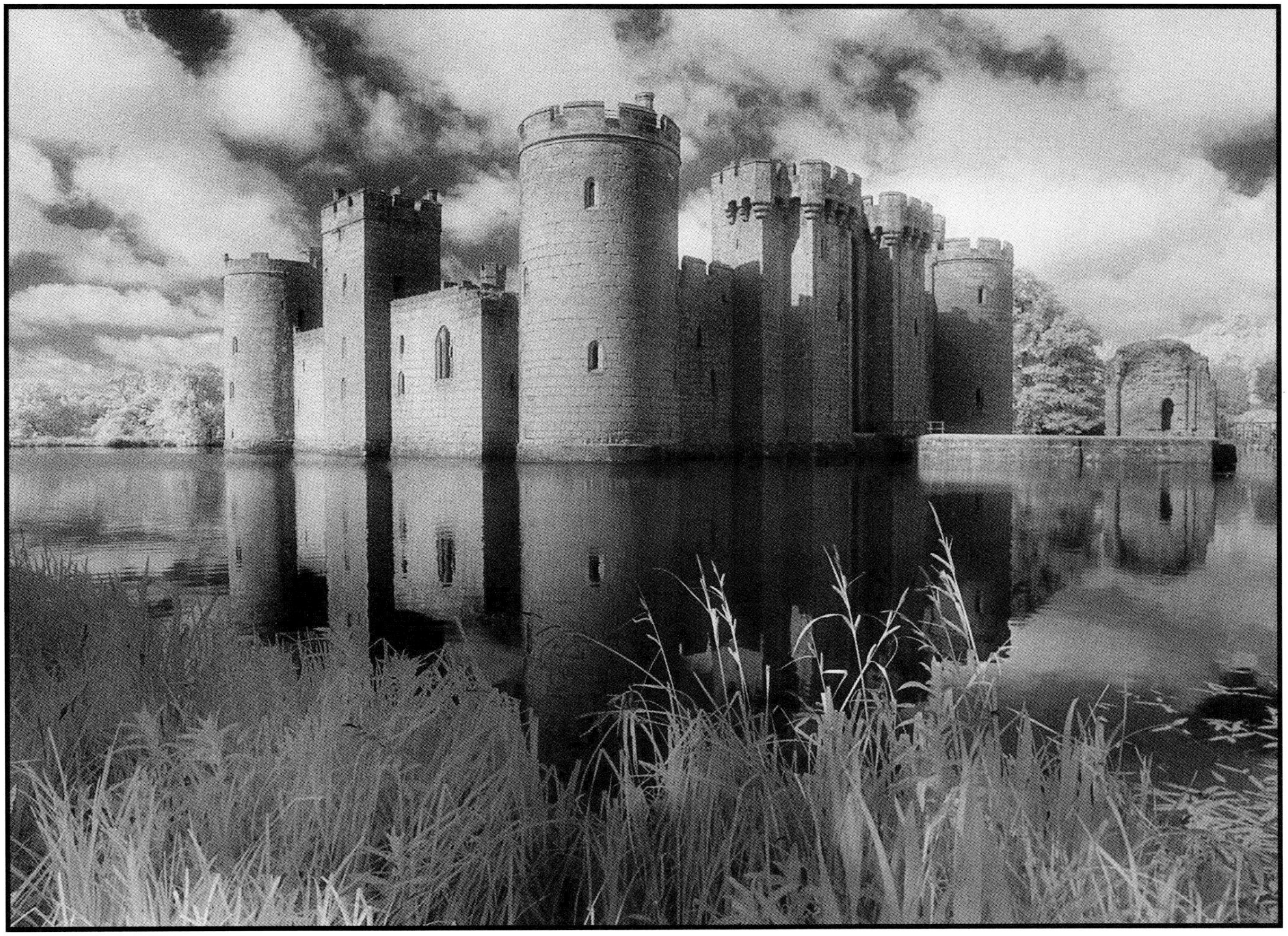

THE PHOTOGRAPHY OF
KATHY HARCOM

rm

AREM PHOTOGRAPHY PORTFOLIOS

LIGHT SENSITIVE
Kathy Harcom

Arem Photography Portfolios #1
Published in the UK by Arem Publishing Ltd
20 St Peters Road, Croydon, CR0 1HD

British Library Cataloguing-in-Publication Data:
A catalogue record for the book is available from the British Library.

ISBN 1-904825-01-X
First edition, 2004

Printed in Italy by Graphic Studio, Verona.

For details of other books and magazines published by Arem Publishing Ltd and of our mail order business for photographic products and materials, please visit our website:
www.arempublishing.co.uk or write to us at the address given above.

INTRODUCTION

THIS BOOK IS DEDICATED TO
THE MEMORY OF MY WONDERFUL MUM, BERNICE ROSE
AND TO HUSBAND PETE AND CHILDREN, BEN AND JENNY

Light Sensitive is my first book and I am delighted to have the opportunity to share my portfolio with you. There are also three introductory essays on the main photographic techniques I use: infrared photography, lith printing and hand colouring. These are not intended as technical treatises, but I hope they will be enough to get anyone started who is interested in exploring these techniques for themselves.

My approach to taking the pictures has evolved since I first started taking colour transparencies in the late 1980s. My main purpose at that time was to record important moments that happen in family life, always conscious that little things are all too easily forgotten. But as I became more interested in the creative side of photography, I began to take courses and workshops and attend exhibitions. All of which opened my eyes to more possibilities and were to be a turning point in my photography.

Starting to use black and white film was a real discovery. I was immediately captivated. Not only did the purity and simplicity of the medium draw me, but my fascination became complete when I learned to print my own work. Watching the image materialise in front of me in the developing dish was magical. Creative control was suddenly within my grasp, from the moment I pressed the shutter to the time I held the print in my hands; the possibilities for personal expression seemed limitless.

Discovering my favourite film was another special moment. As soon as I printed my first roll of Kodak Infrared film I knew I had discovered something that perfectly matched the way I like to interpret my subjects. Soft, delicate, ethereal images with an almost otherworldly feel became possible with this extended sensitivity film. Most of the pictures in this book are taken with this lovely film.

In general the majority of my pictures are unplanned. I prefer to work intuitively, responding to what I see and feel. I am sensitive to the quality of light and the interplay between this and my subjects and it is often the light that inspires me to pick up the camera. I strive to make images that evoke a sense of tranquillity and capture the heart and soul of a special place or a forgotten corner.

I am not too precious about equipment and have for many years used an Olympus OM2N camera with its superb Zuiko lenses (21mm, 28mm, 50mm and 75-150 lenses are my collection). Although now 23 years old, and despite a slightly dodgy wind-on lever, it continues to serve me well. Three pictures in the still life section were taken on a Bronica ETRSi with a 75mm lens, but the remainder were taken on the Olympus.

Many people have inspired, encouraged and supported me along the way to making my pictures and this book, and to them I am very grateful. I wanted to give special thanks to Ronnie Bennett and Miranda Duncan, my artistic soul mates, and to John Philpott, Roger Maile, Bob Elliott, Tim Rudman and the members of Arena and Chimera for all their encouragement over the years.

CONTENTS

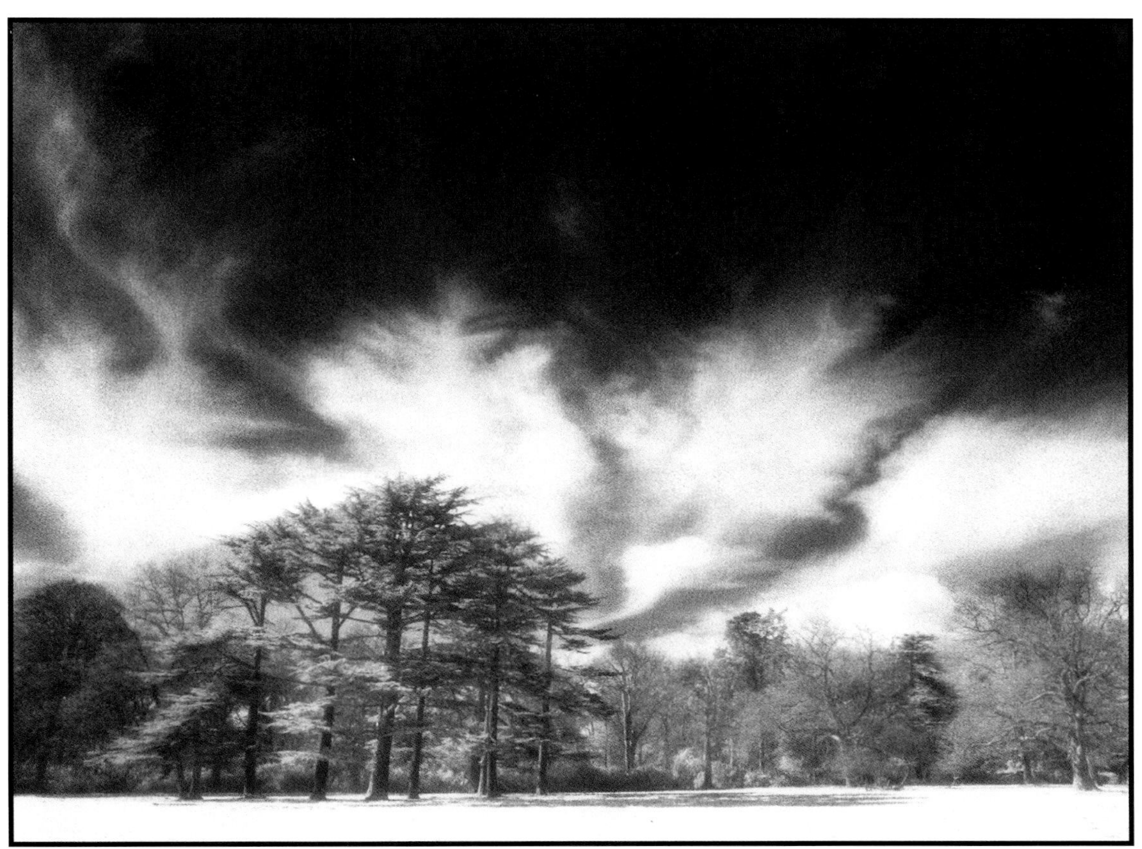

Stormy sky
This print was made from the first roll of infrared (Kodak HIE) I ever used.

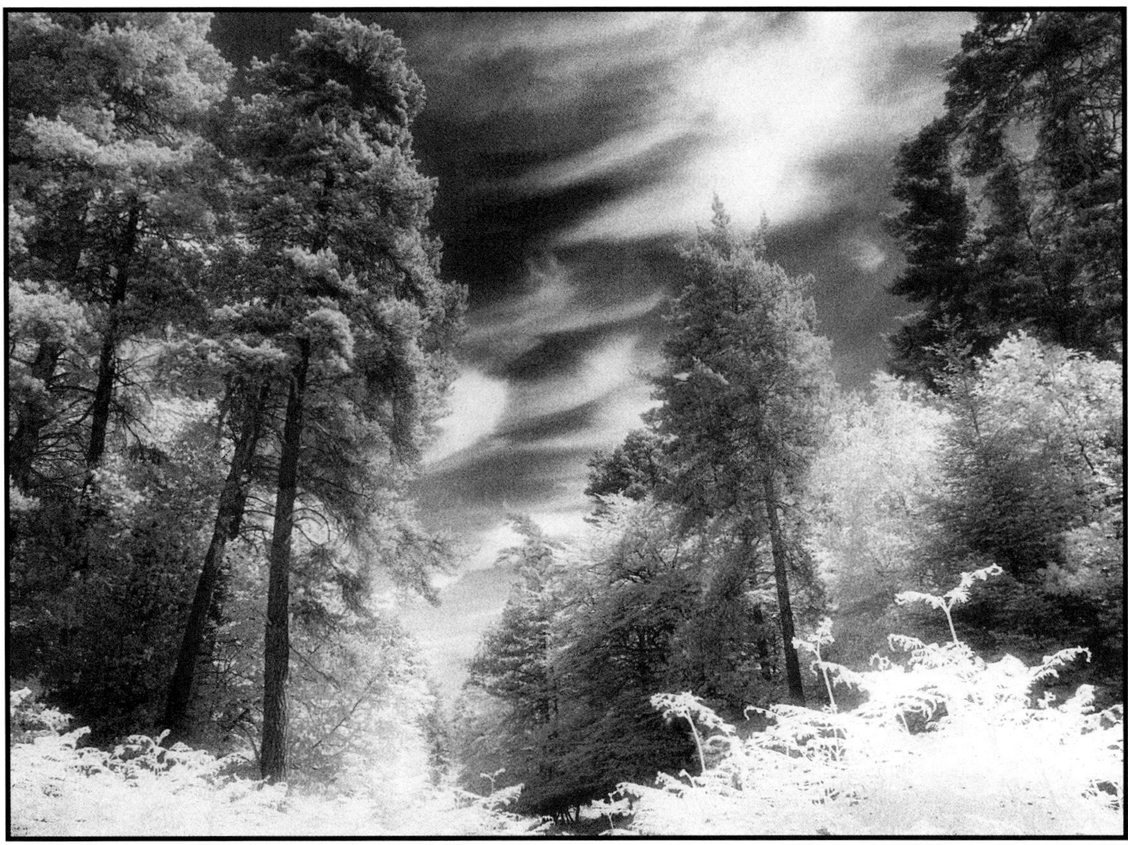

Skydancers

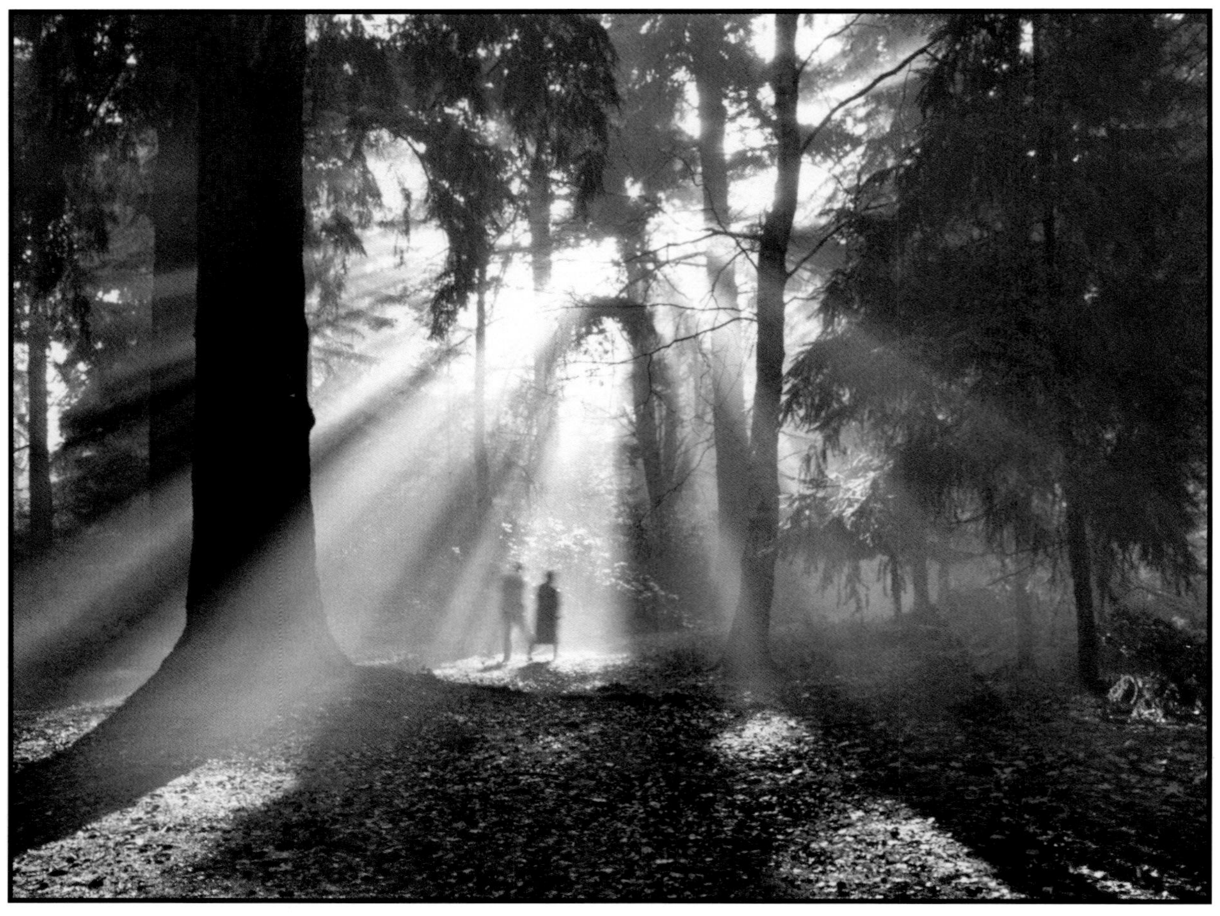

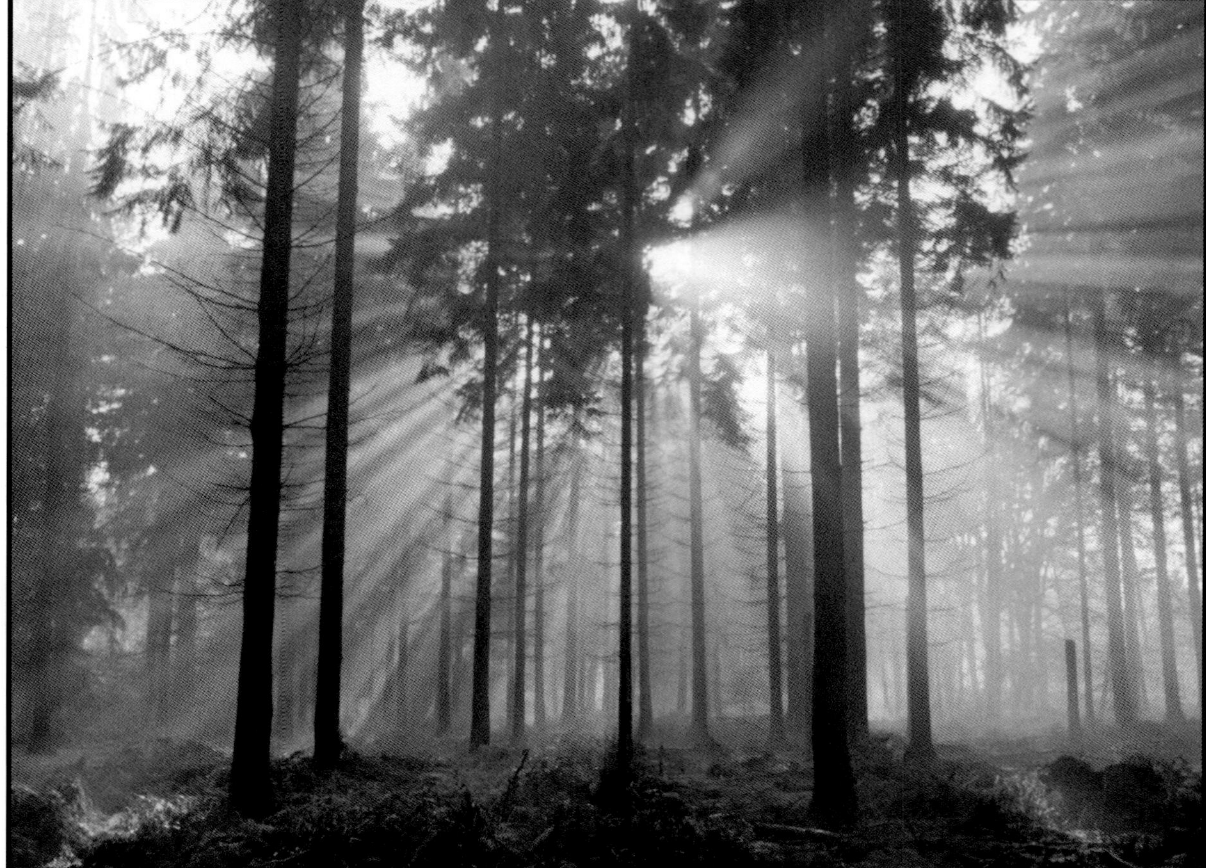

(top left)
The visitors

(bottom left)
Boldrewood

(right)
Harmony

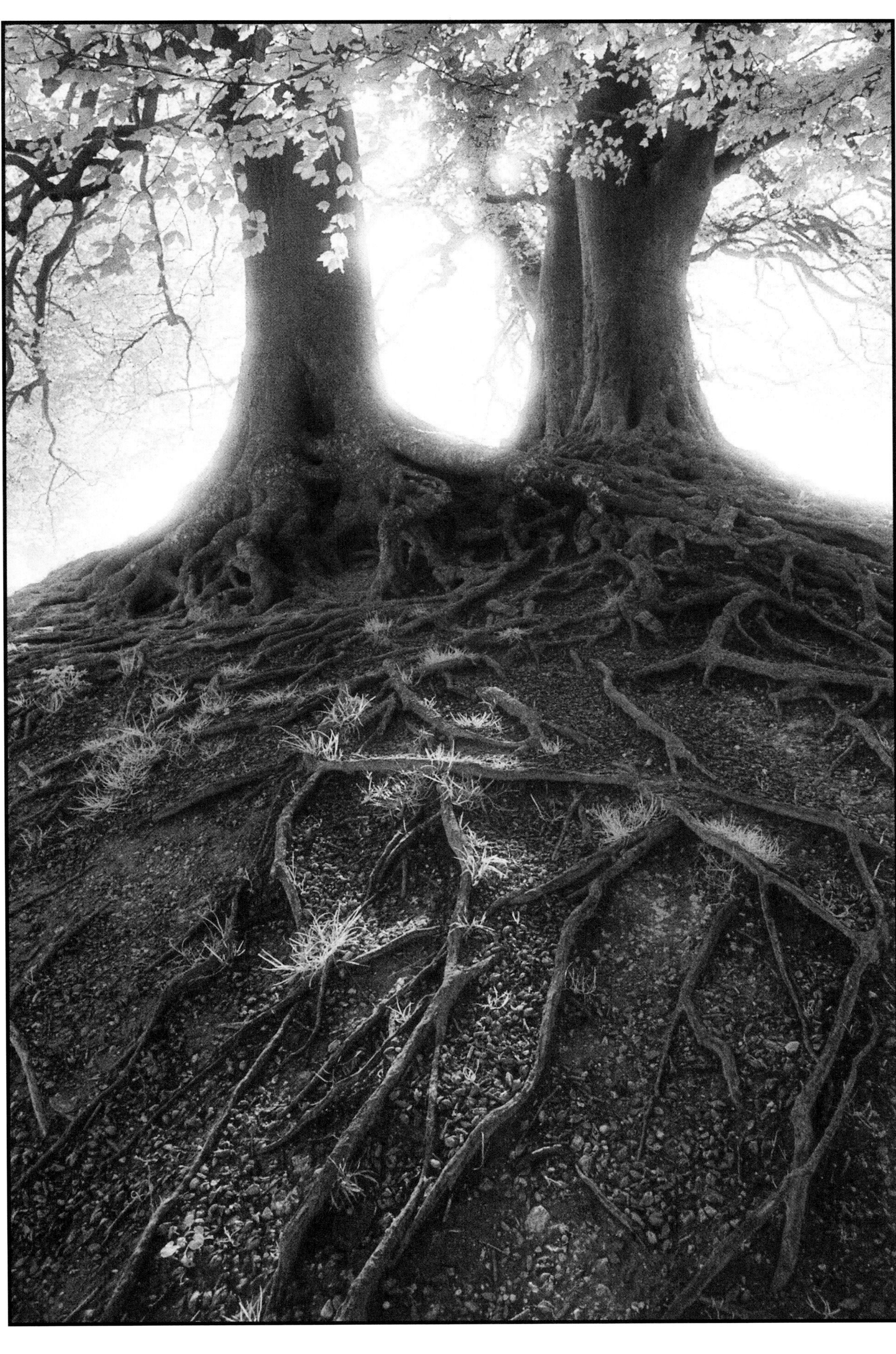

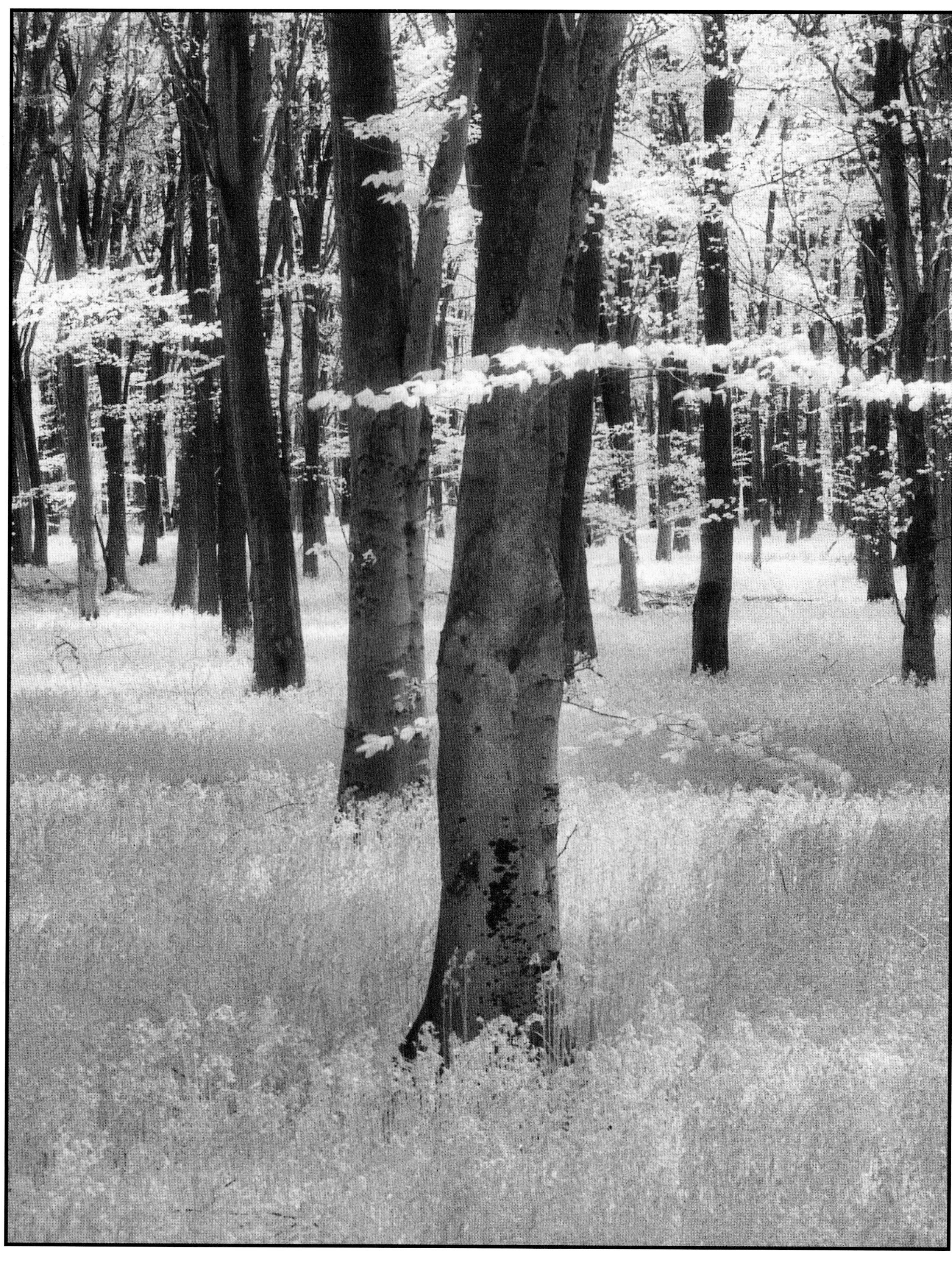

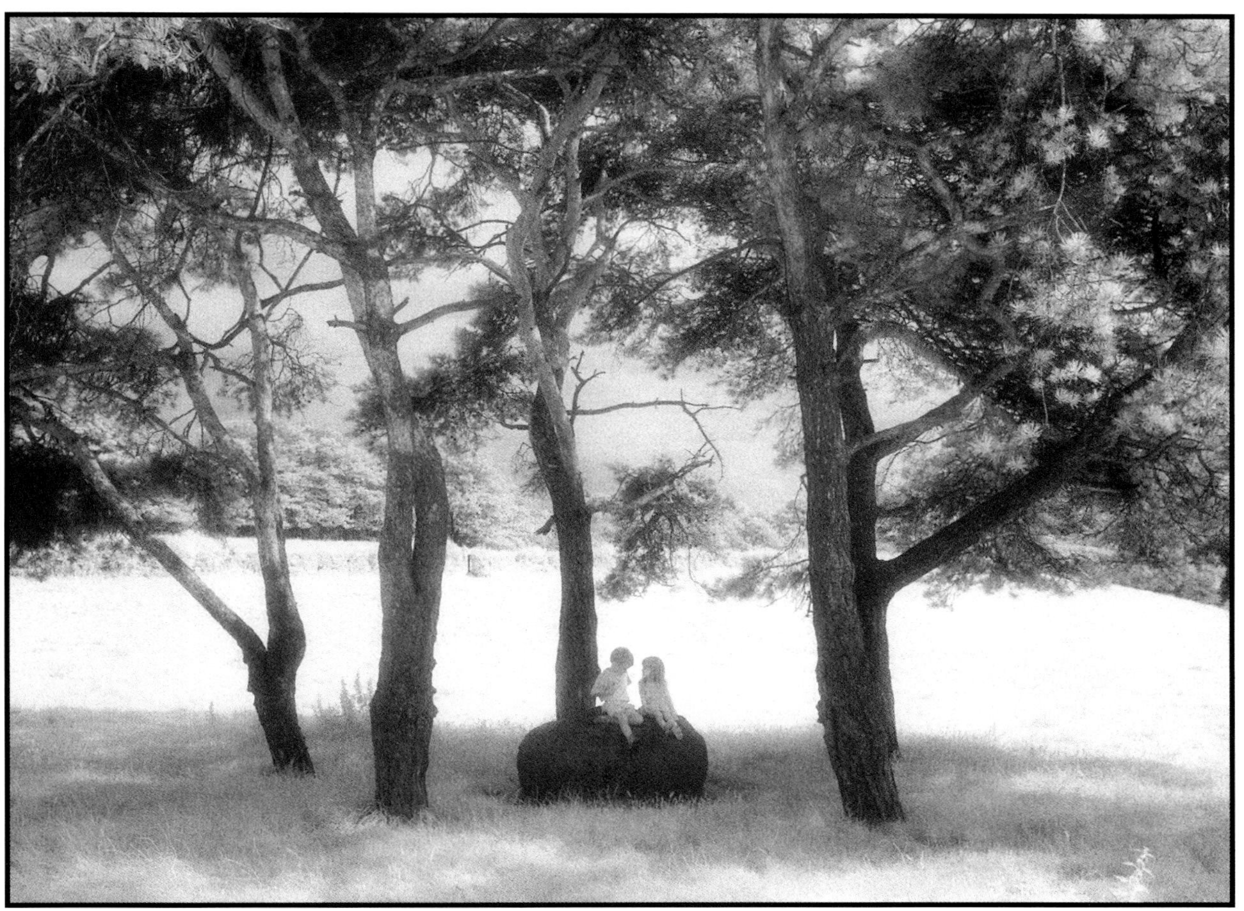

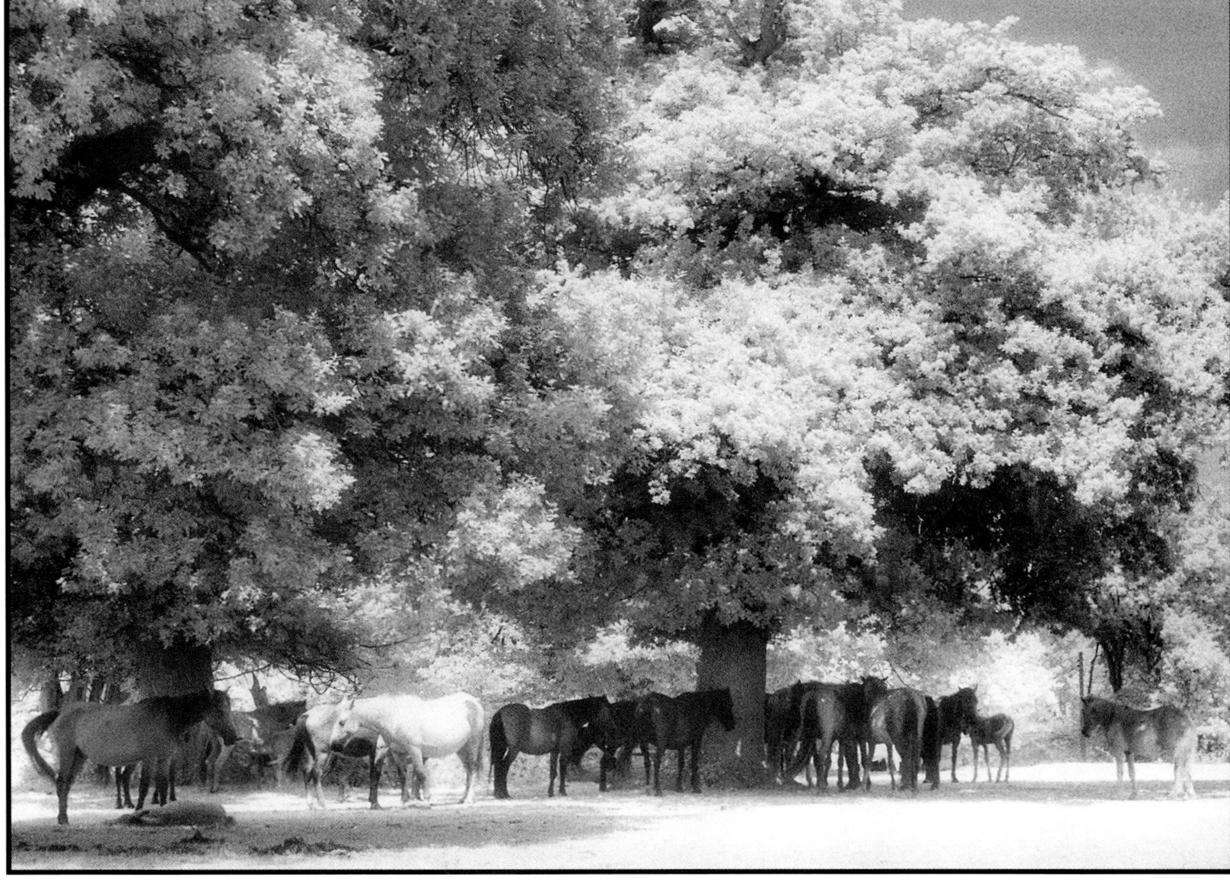

(left)
Bluebell Wood

(top right)
Memories

(bottom right)
The Gathering

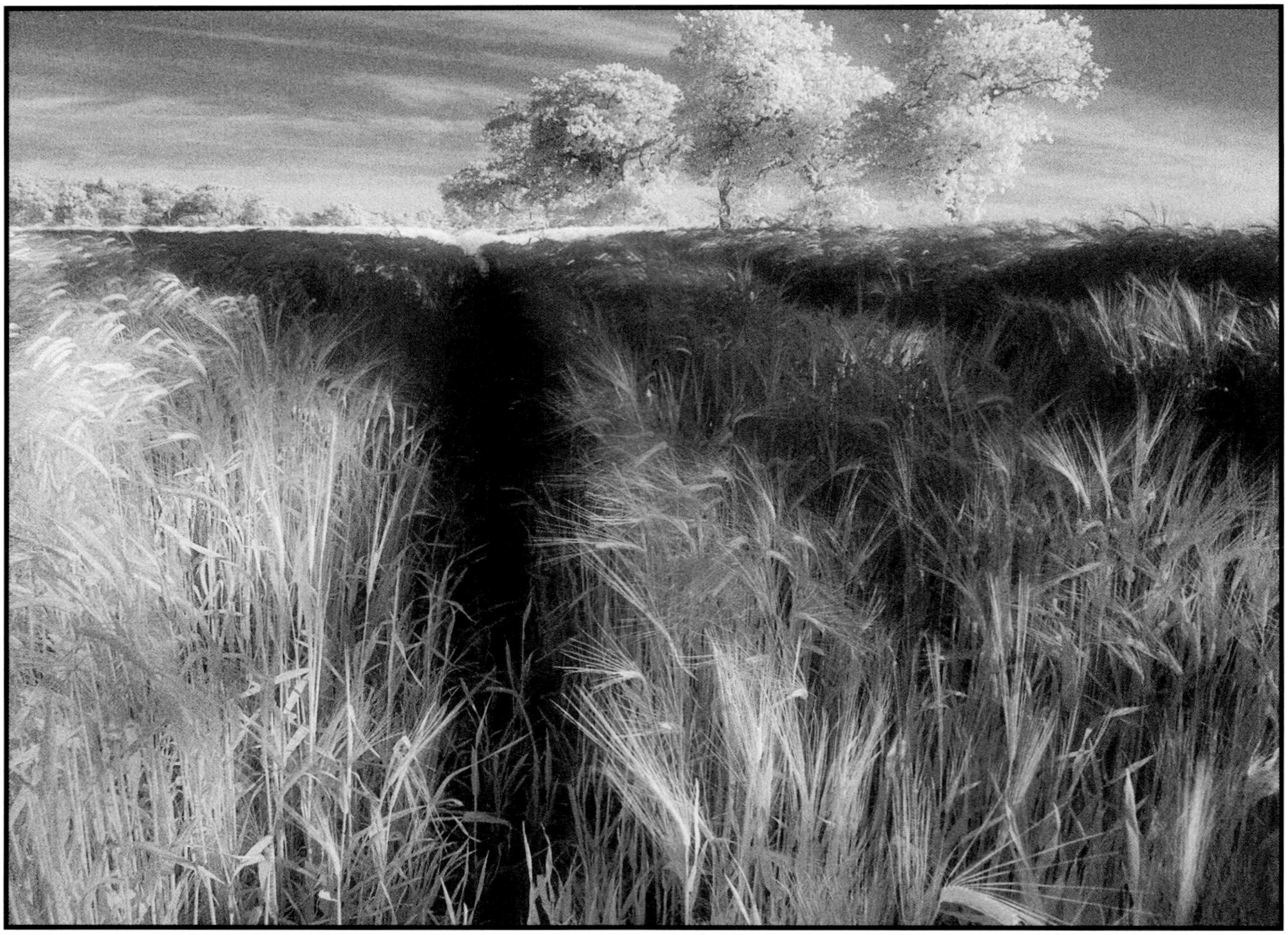

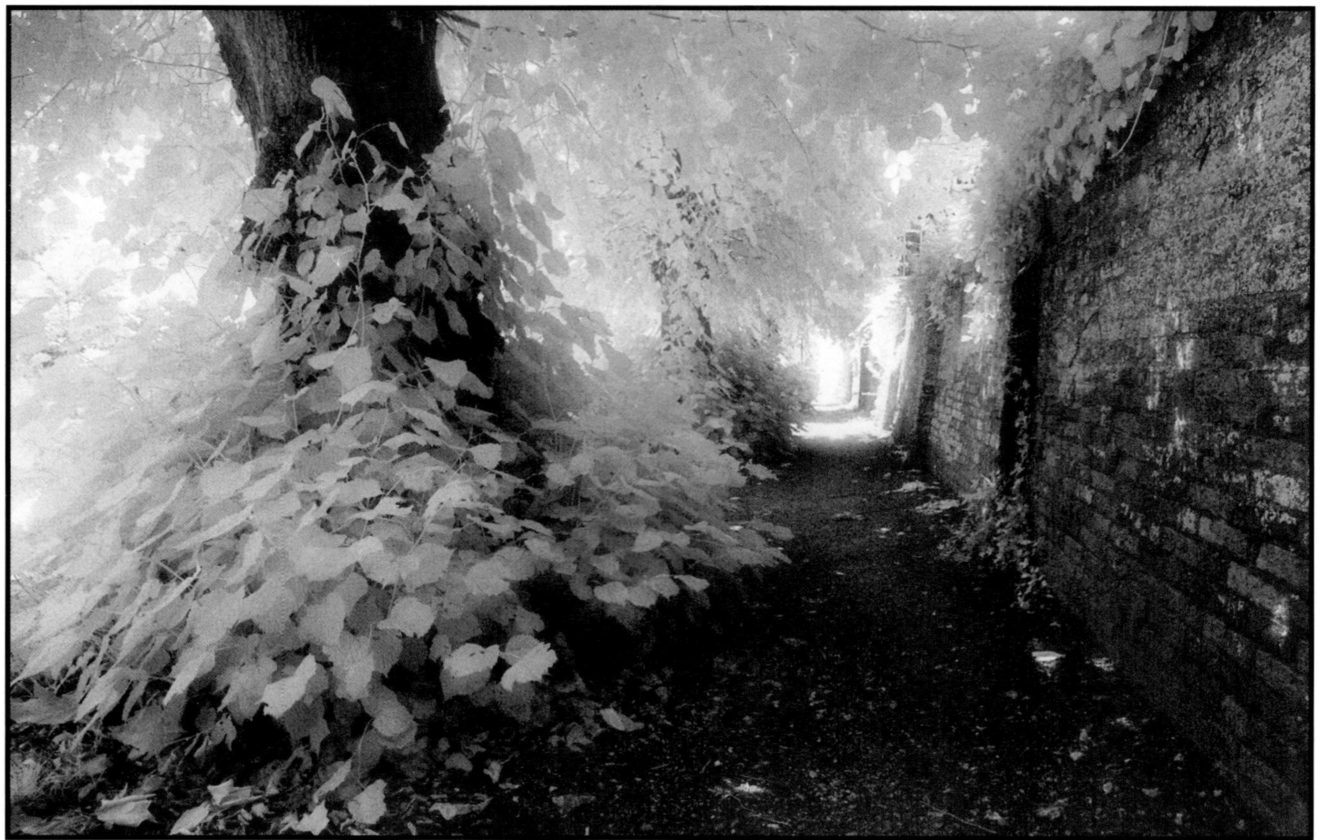

(top left)
Barley field

(bottom left)
Walkway

(right)
Path

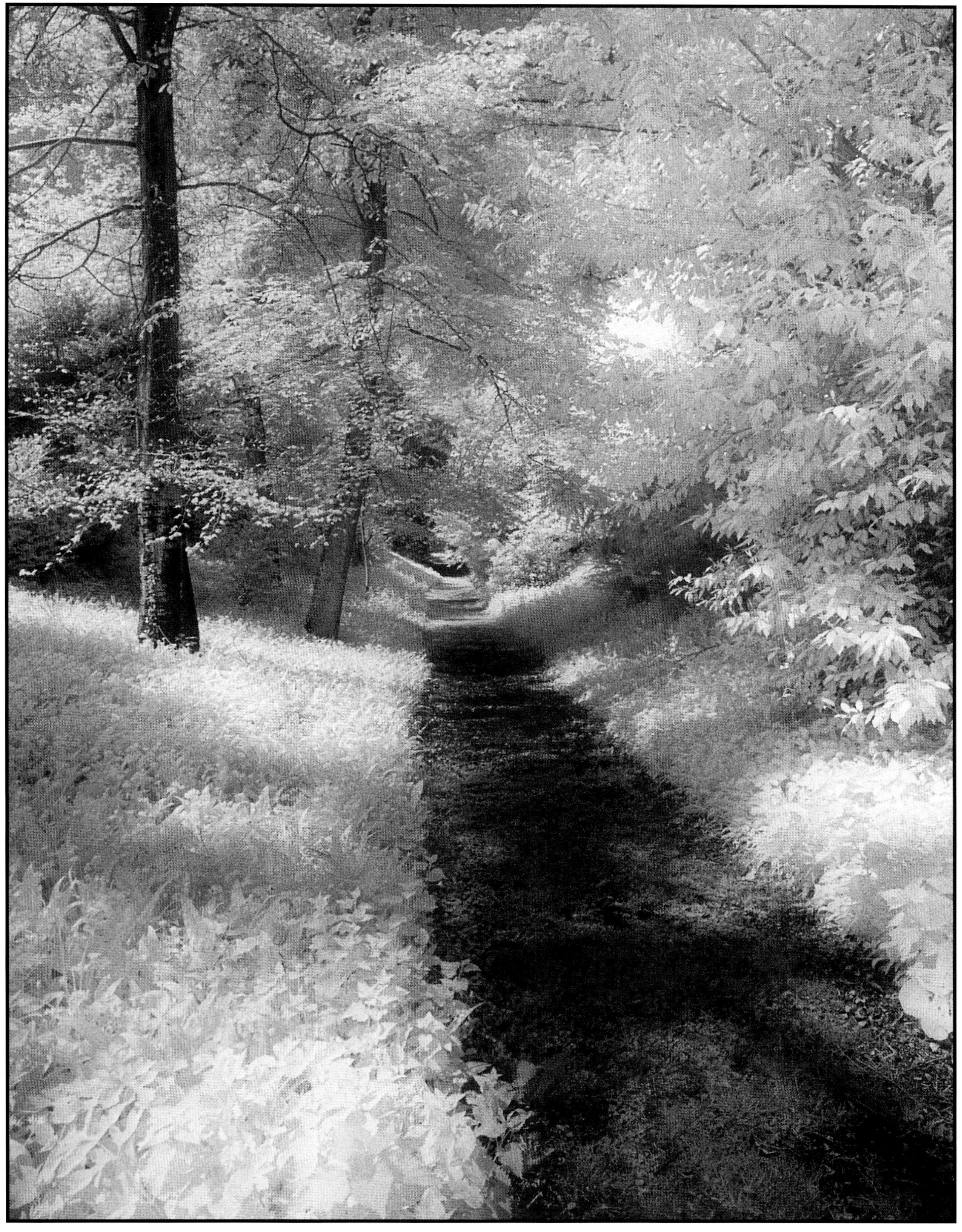

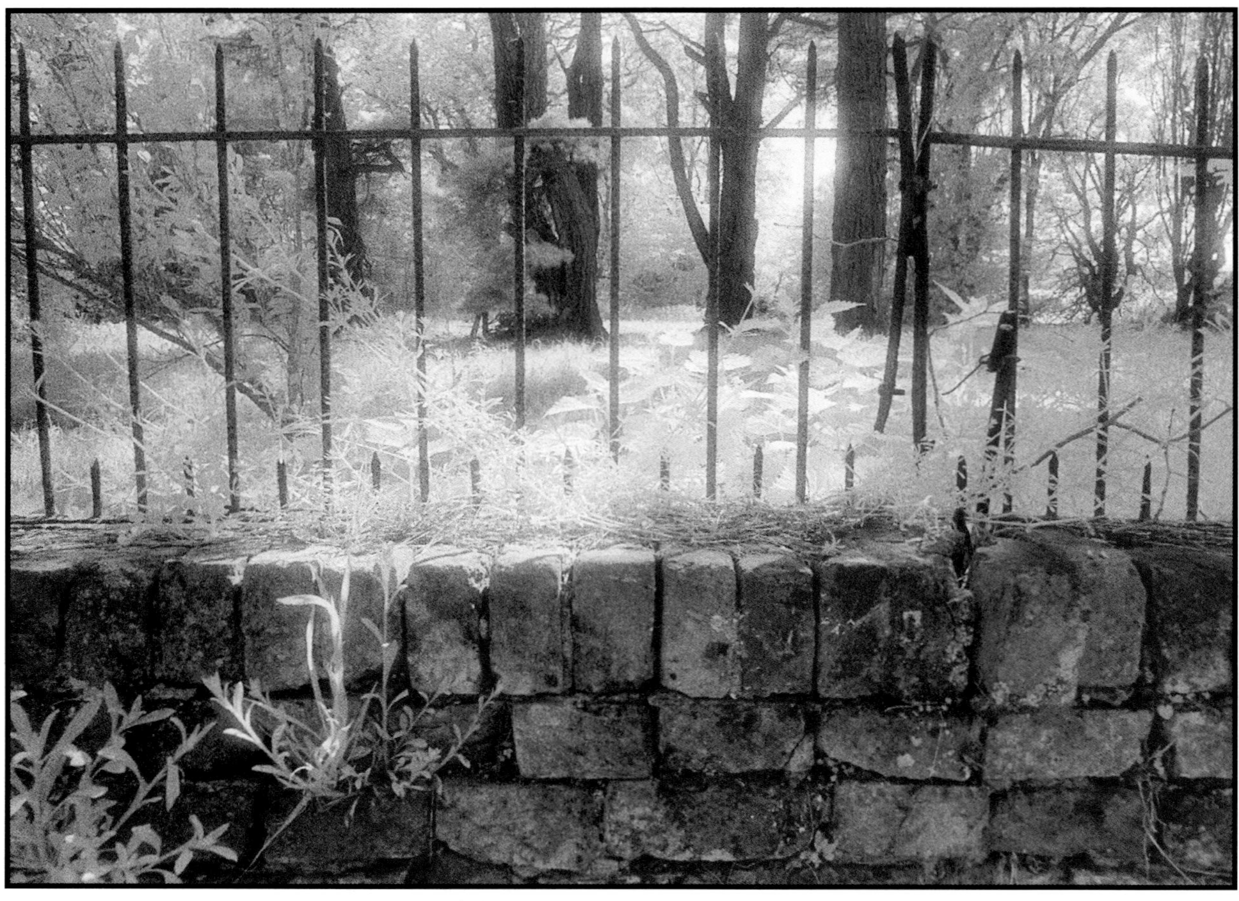

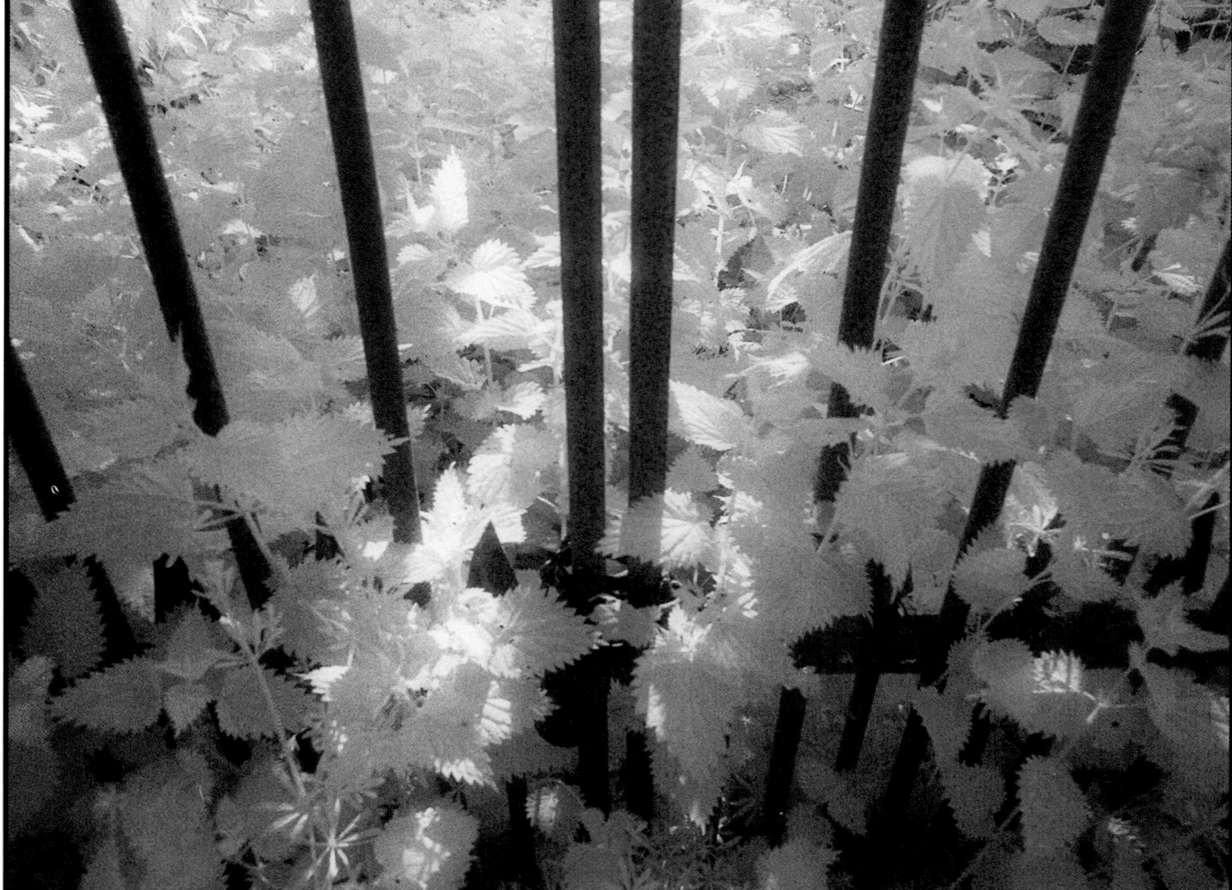

(top left)
Secret forest

(bottom left)
The gate

(right)
Closed

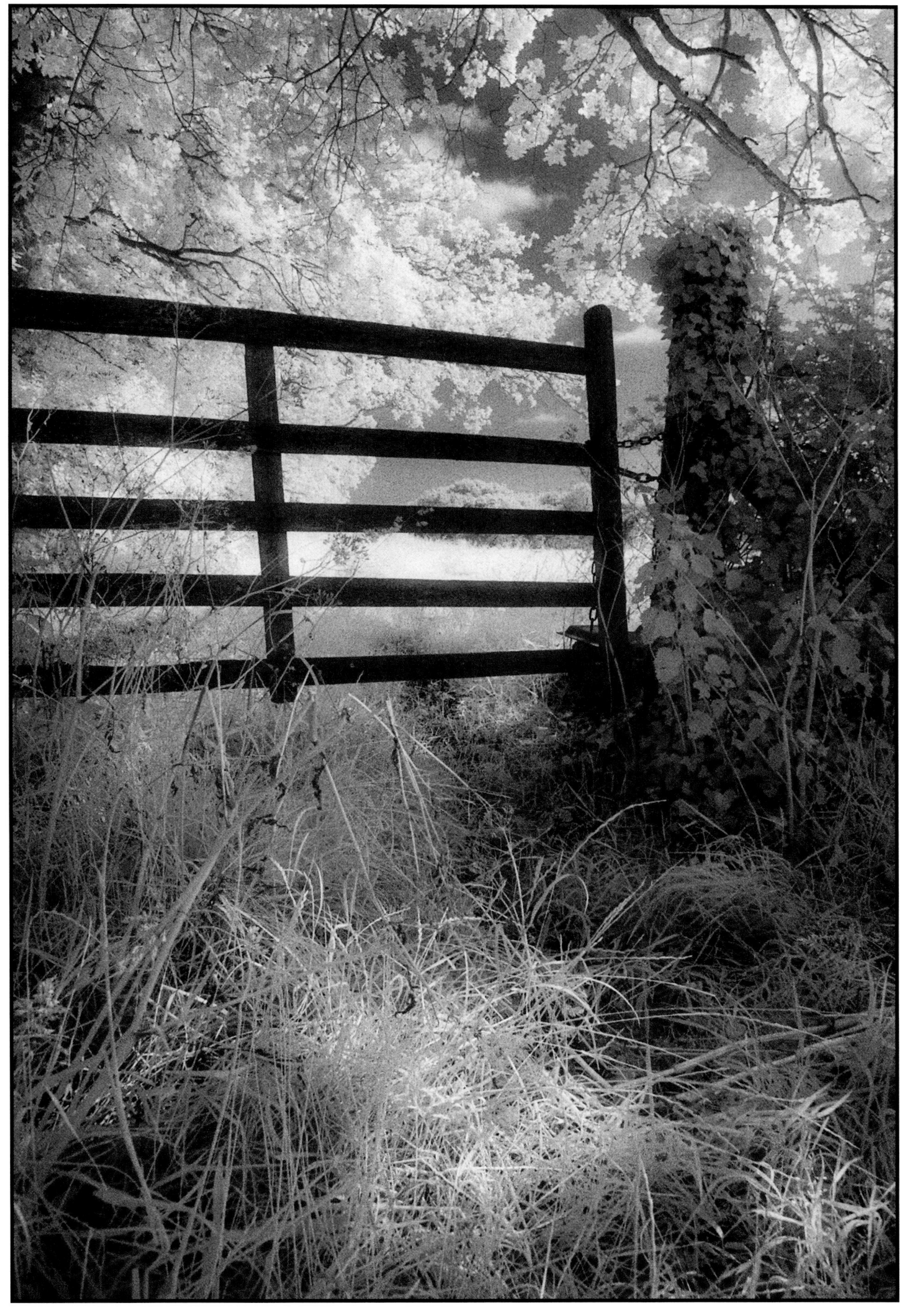

SEEING THE INVISIBLE

Virtually all of my personal photography is made using black and white infrared film. This introduction is intended to help those who want to use this type of film for the first time.

Infrared films have a special emulsion that responds to a wider range of light and radiant energy than normal films. They are capable of 'seeing' into the invisible and recording images not normally seen by the eyes. Although these films require special handling, the results more than make up for the extra effort and care involved in their use. Infrared images can be stunning, almost other-worldly and immensely beautiful.

How things will record depends largely on what you photograph, the weather conditions and the filtration you use. In good light, live, healthy foliage both transmits and reflects a lot of near-infrared. These subjects record as dense areas on your negative and once printed are almost white, as though covered in snow: fluffy looking and luminous. In contrast, open skies and bodies of water that reflect no infrared record as thin areas on the negative and print very dark: bold and dramatic. Pictures of people look unusual with skin tones appearing pale, lips bleached and eyes dark. This shift in tonal range is what makes infrared images stand out. IR films also cut through atmospheric haze in distant landscapes and can be used after dark.

There are currently four different monochrome infrared films available to photographers and these are described in the panel opposite. This brief guide refers to the most sensitive of the films: Kodak HIE, High speed infrared film. This is my favourite infrared film and the one that offers the most dramatic effects.

FILTRATION

The emulsion layer in IR films will record both visible light and near infrared, so a picture taken without filtration would appear quite unspectacular. To exploit the film's special characteristics, the visible light needs to be blocked, leaving only red and near infrared to be recorded. A number of filters are suitable; the two I use are Hoya Red 25A and Hoya Infrared R72.

Hoya Red 25A will block UV, blue and green, but will admit red and near infrared. It is very effective with Kodak HIE and has the benefit of allowing visual focusing and composition. This is my preferred filter and the one I use most of the time.

Hoya Infrared R72 produces a slightly stronger infrared effect, knocking out UV, blue, green and red, leaving only the near infrared to record. It is however more tricky to use. Being visually opaque, focusing becomes impossible once the filter is in place and so needs to be done before the filter is attached to the lens.

Even stronger results can be achieved using the opaque Wratten 87 and 87C filters. (Lesser strength filters, orange, etc, will not give very interesting results.)

EXPOSURE

Unlike normal films, true infrared films have no film speed rating. Light meters measure visible light and are not calibrated to record infrared accurately. So metered readings cannot be regarded as being precise, but they can be used as a guide.

I have found success using the following combinations. During bright, warm, sunny summer conditions with a Hoya 25A filter over the lens, I set a film speed rating of 400 ISO and allow the TTL metering in the camera to find a starting point. During the cooler but bright days of Spring and Autumn, I reset to 200 ISO, and during cooler overcast days, I reset to 100 ISO.

These settings provide the starting point from which I then 'bracket' my exposures. The number of extra exposures I make is usually in direct proportion to how much time and trouble I have had in getting to a particular place and setting up a photograph and whether it is an unrepeatable event. In 'lots of trouble' cases, I would take the indicated exposure then +1, +2 and -1, -2 stops – so 5 pictures in all. At less precious times, I would just take the indicated exposure and one stop either side.

ANTI-HALATION LAYER AND FILM LOADING

There is no anti-halation layer on Kodak HIE. This opaque layer is normally added to films to prevent the scatter effect caused by light going through the film base and then being reflected back onto the emulsion. This happens when there are strong highlights causing a secondary image to form as it re-enters the emulsion. The absence of this layer in Kodak HIE allows these imperfections to manifest themselves resulting in the distinctive glowing halos in the highlights.

This also affects the way film should be loaded or removed from the camera. It cannot be loaded or removed unless in a darkroom or changing bag, otherwise the film leader will act as a 'light pipe' drawing-in light along the surface and fogging the film.

STORAGE

Film should be stored in the refrigerator or freezer in the original packaging. Before use, allow the film to return to room temperature – otherwise condensation can form on the film causing unwanted, unpleasant special effects.

Very high temperatures will fog the film slightly and produce inferior results, but it will cope with normal changes in temperature. The entire film doesn't need shooting at one time: just ensure partly exposed film is stored in a cool place. Pop the camera in a storage place at 55°F or lower if possible.

EQUIPMENT AND TROUBLESHOOTING

Equipment you are planning to use needs to be opaque to IR radiation. If in doubt, run a test film through the camera and/or processing equipment before taking any important pictures. Some cameras are unsuitable for IR photography, eg those that rely on IR devices to assist film loading and frame counting – this can cause fogging on film rebates and invade the image area. Cameras that rely solely on auto-focus are not best suited either as they do not allow for manual correction (see 'Focusing' below).

Cameras with dimpled pressure plates will cause problems with Kodak HIE. Without the anti-halation layer, light bouncing back off the dimples shows up as a regular circular pattern, often only noticed in large even toned areas like skies. This can be solved by fitting a smooth pressure plate, if available, or a crude solution is to cover the dimpled plate with black fablon type material.

FOCUSING

IR focuses at a different point to visible light. In practice this is slightly nearer than for visible light. Most lenses have a small red mark on the focusing ring, which shows the adjustment. However, if you have no adjustment on your lens, do not despair: it is not a huge difference and only becomes critical when the subject is close to the camera and a longer focal lens is used. Wide-angle lenses stopped down to a small aperture cope well.

PROCESSING

Film should be loaded in complete darkness into an infrared safe processing tank. Once loaded, processing can be done in normal lighting. I use a standard developer, either Kodak D76 or Ilford ID11 (although there are many other suitable developers). I use a stock solution for 11 minutes at 20°C in a small tank, agitating continuously for the first 30 seconds and then once every minute (5 inversions), followed by a brief stop bath of 30 seconds and then a fix of between 2 and 4 minutes depending on the fixer involved. I wash the film for at least 15-20 minutes at a reasonable temperature (say ±5°C of the processing temperature).

PRINTING YOUR IMAGES

If you have bracketed your exposures, you should have a good choice of negatives to print from. Looking at your contact sheet, choose to print the frames where the 'black' in the scene matches the black of the film base (viewable on the film rebates) with a density similar to normal negatives.

Assuming you have taken your pictures with a suitable filter in place you will notice a change in tonal values as compared with standard panchromatic film. This shift may take a little getting used to and can be further enhanced by careful printing and dodging/burning-in of selected areas.

Don't be afraid to let your highlight areas glow and sparkle: the brightest highlight can be as bright as the paper base. Areas like ponds, lakes and deep blue skies will be very dark: celebrate these differences!

Later, you can revisit the remaining negatives. Printing from a variety of densities will reveal different characteristics. Dense negatives show a rapid increase in grain and reduced tonal separation. These negatives will interpret as ghostly, grainy and dramatic. Thin negatives have a finer grain structure, delicate and bright.

Kodak HIE has many moods and how this is expressed will be largely down to your interpretation. There is really no 'right way' or 'wrong way' to expose and print your negatives: just do what feels right for you and aim to achieve what you want from your pictures. With experience and experimentation, results become much more controllable, but there is always an element of unpredictability about infrared photography which makes it all the more interesting and exciting.

FILMS AVAILABLE

There are four monochrome films currently available which are suitable for infrared and extended-red photography. The most important differences are their levels of sensitivity, and therefore the degree to which they can record in the near infrared region.

Kodak HIE High Speed Infrared film, which is the most sensitive of the four, with a spectral sensitivity extending up to 900nm (peak sensitivity between 750-840nm). It has low sensitivity to recording green. The film is fine grain, very sharp and available only in 35mm. The film has no anti-halation layer and must be loaded in complete darkness. Useful filters: Wratten: 25, 89B, 87 and 87C. Good response even with the least strength filter.

Maco IR820c is a fine grain, sharp film. It has peak sensitivity at 820nm and is the closest rival to Kodak for response to infrared. Currently available in 35mm, 120 and 4x5, it has an anti-halation layer (processed out during development leaving a clear base), and should be loaded in total darkness. Useful filters: Wratten: 25, 89B, and 87 – the strongest filter produces the most dramatic response.

Konica Infrared 750 is a slower, very fine grain film, with a sensitivity range up to 820nm (peak 750nm), but it is not sensitive at all to green; currently available both in 35mm and 120 size. It has an anti-halation layer and can be loaded in very subdued light. Useful filters: Wratten: 25 and 89B – strongest filter produces the most dramatic response but lovely tonal rendition with lesser filtration as well.

Ilford SFX 200 ISO film is not a true infrared film and the least sensitive of the four films. It has an extended red sensitivity up to 740nm (peak 720nm). Available both in 35mm and 120 size, it has the benefit of a speed rating, is very easy to handle, it has an anti-halation layer and can be loaded in subdued light. Useful filters: Wratten: 89B and Ilford's own SFX Filter (any lesser strength will not exhibit a particularly unusual response).

SPECTRAL SENSITIVITY

This diagram illustrates the narrow band within the Spectrum that is relevant to photographers. It shows the wavelengths that relate to ultraviolet, visible, and near infrared radiant energy. It also plots a range of film types and compares their sensitivity.

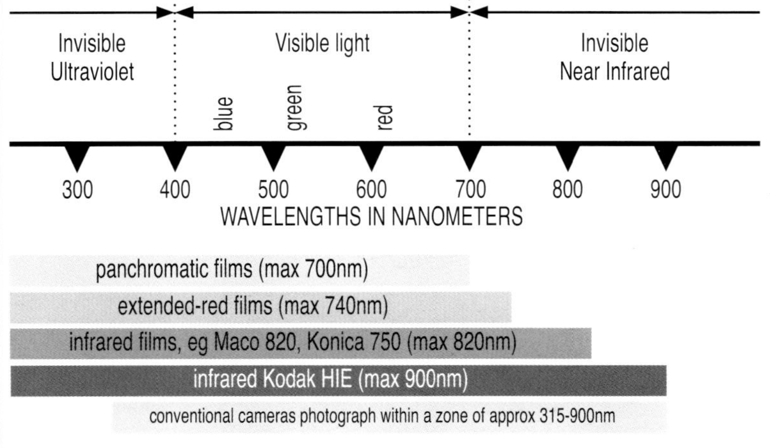

MONOCHROME PORTFOLIO II

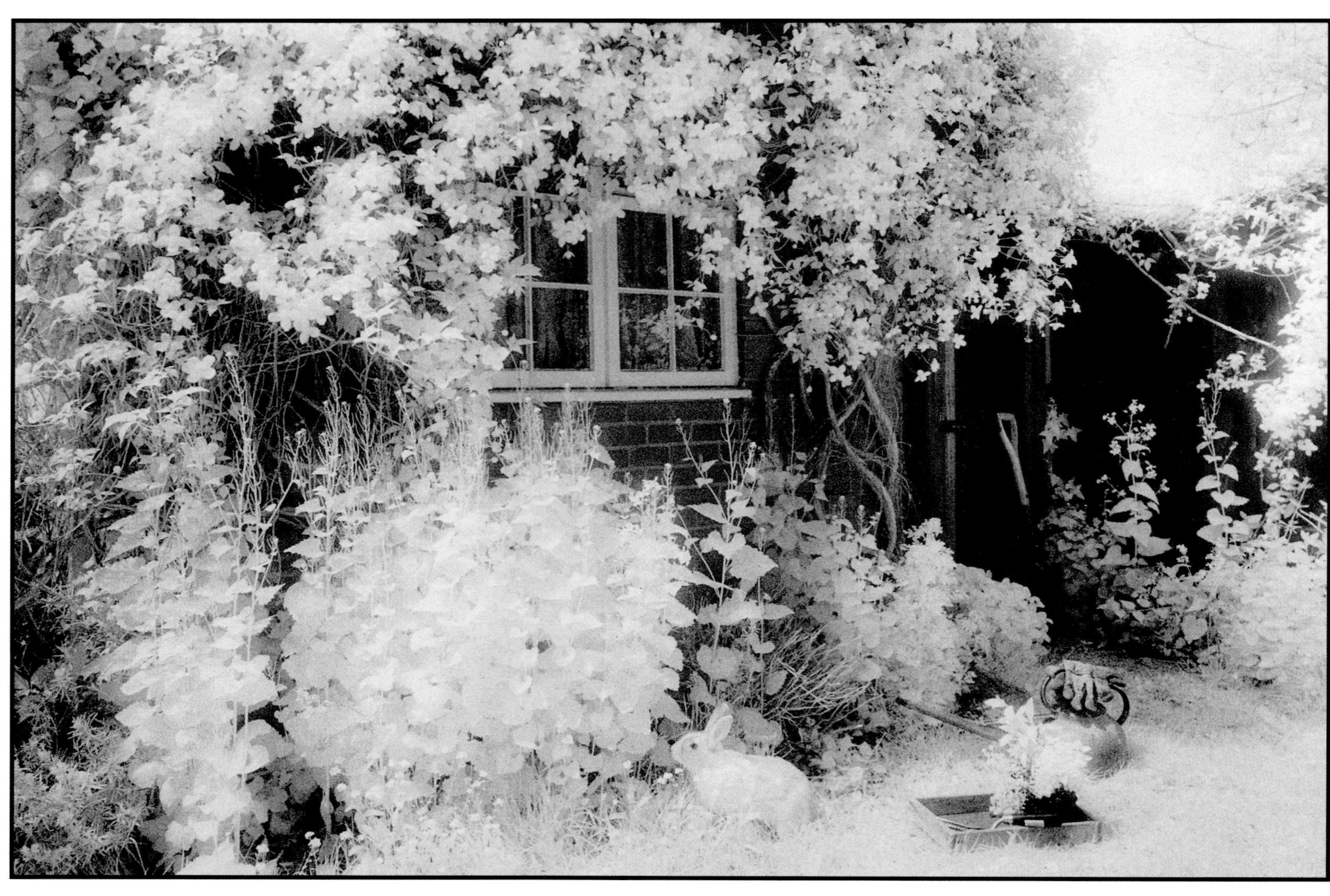

Gardener's place

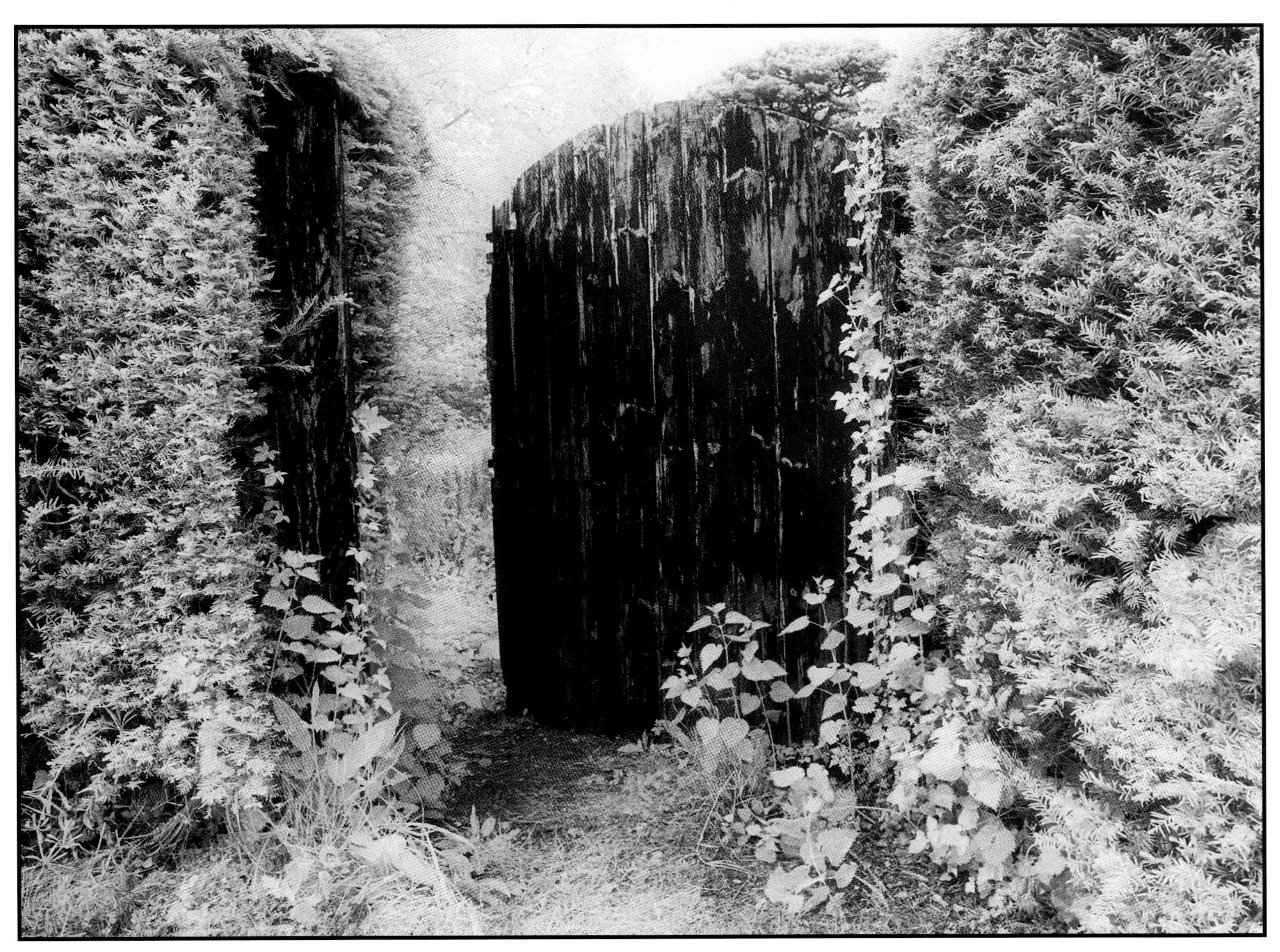

Secret garden

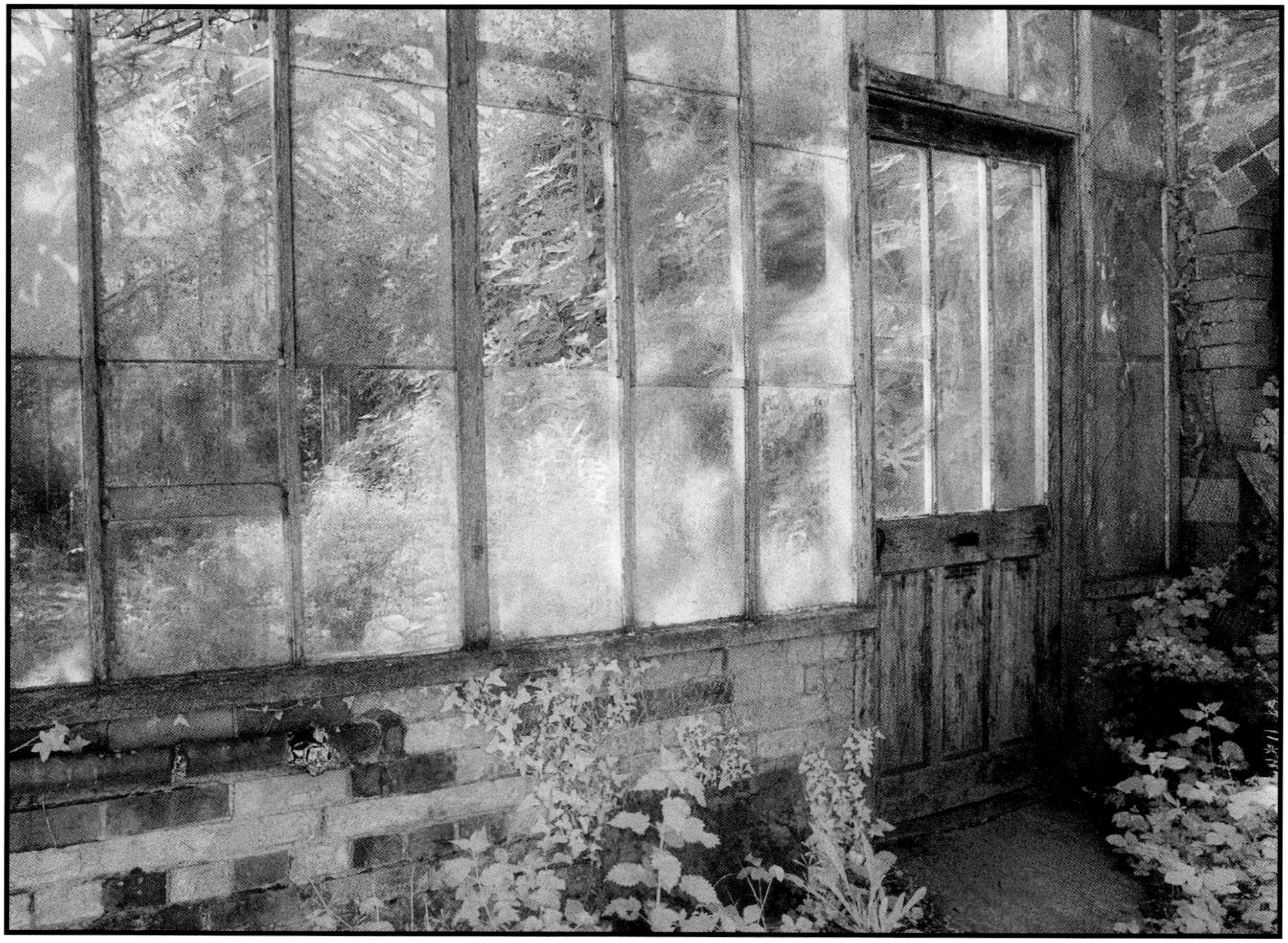

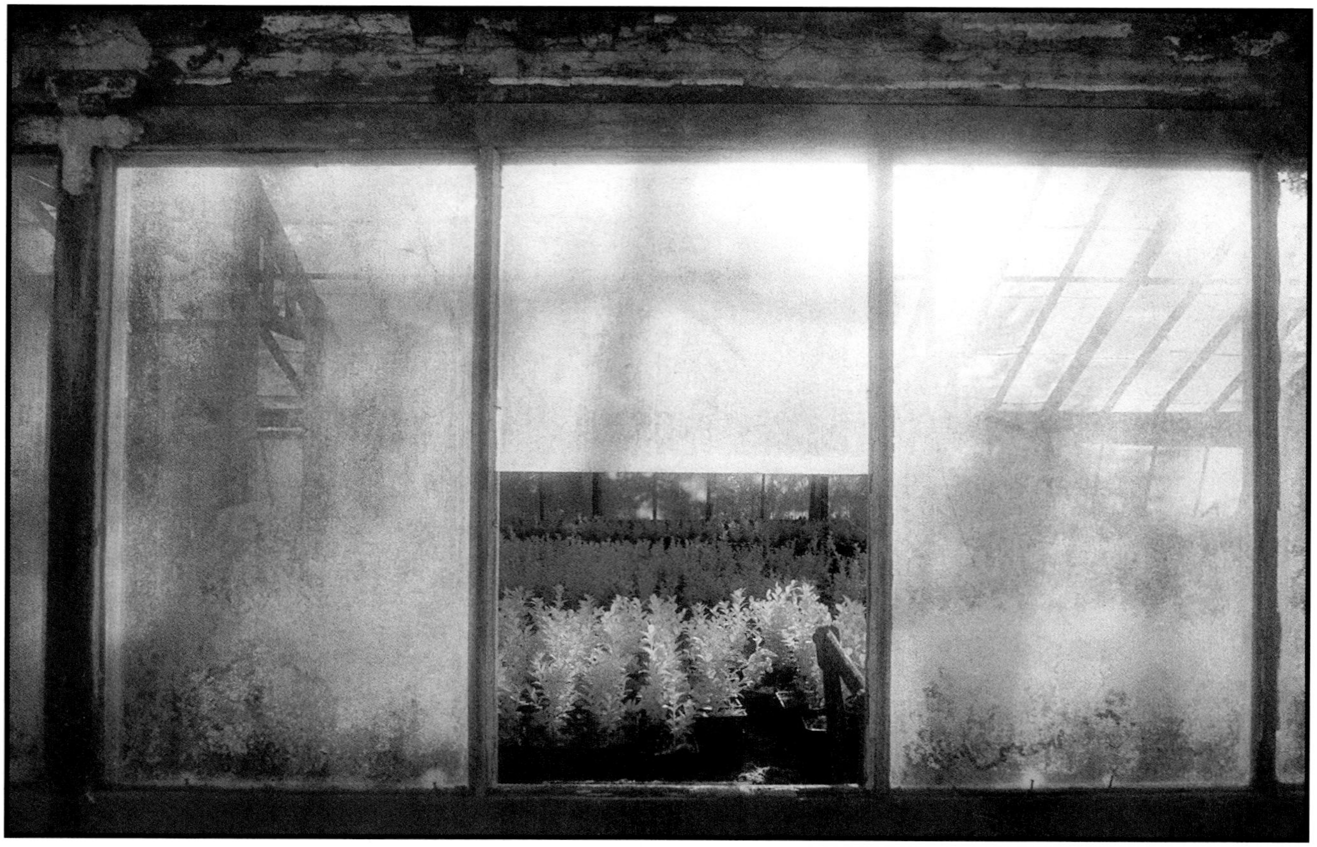

(top left)
The old greenhouse

(bottom left)
Greenhouse window

(right)
Door to the nursery

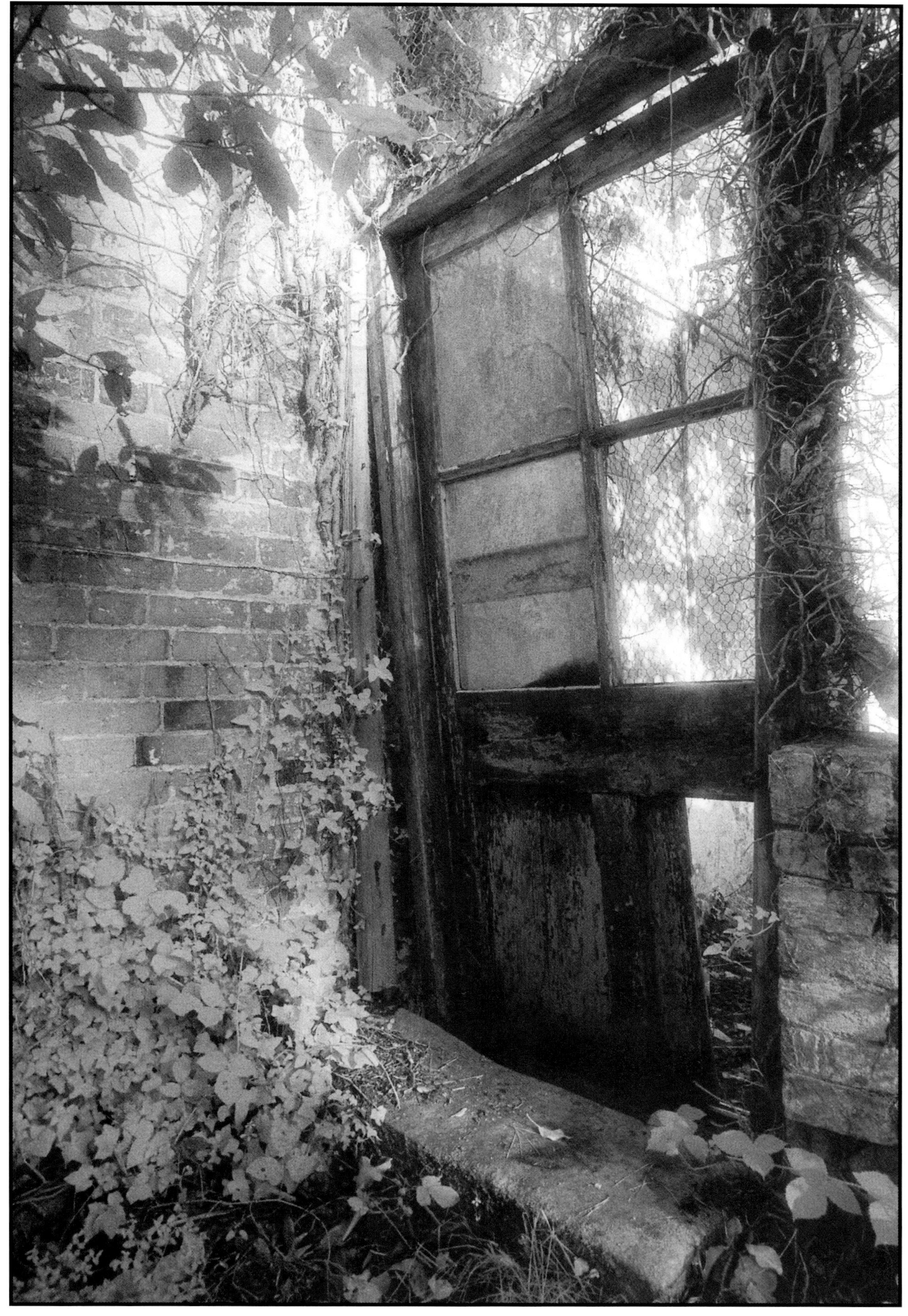

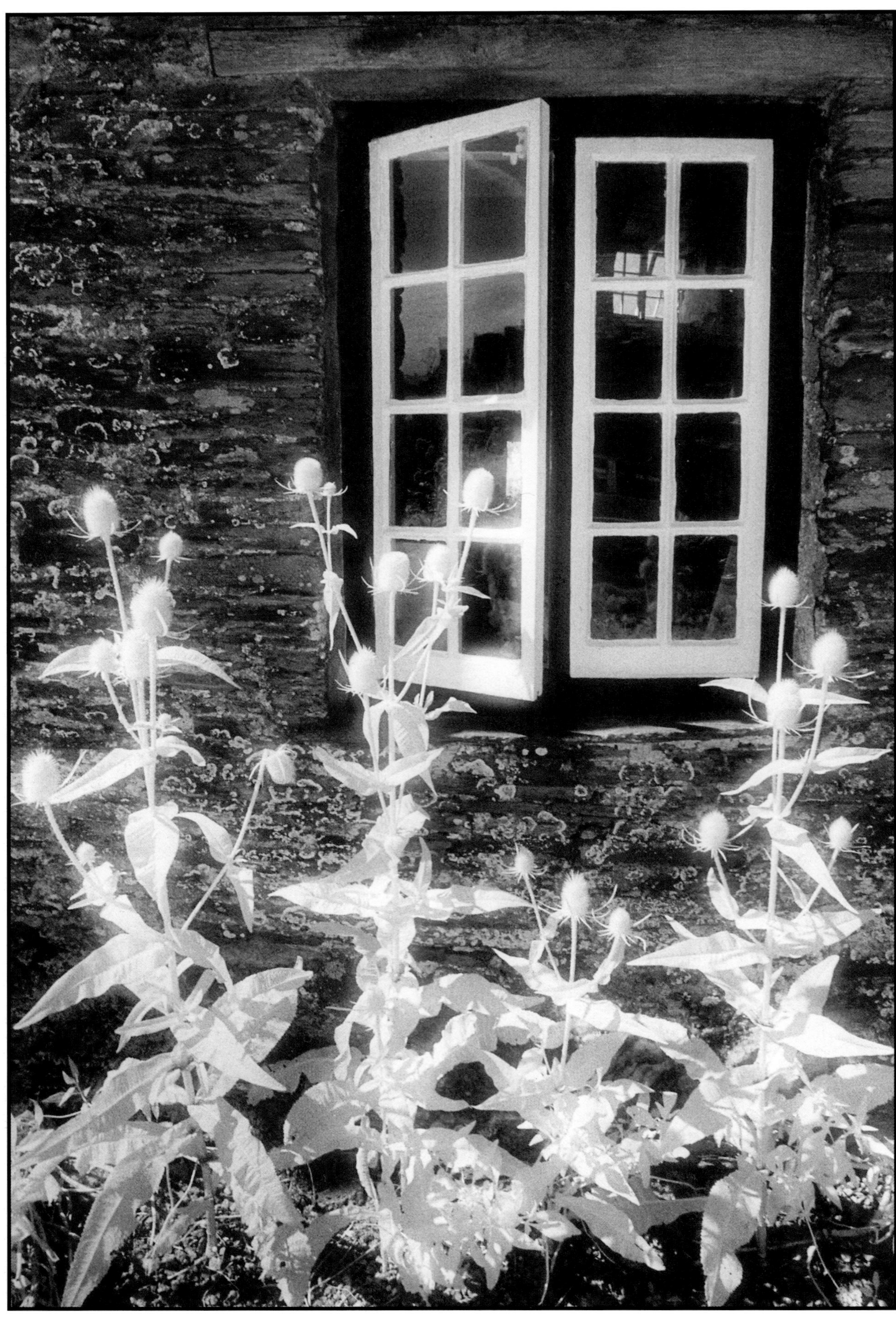

Window with teasels

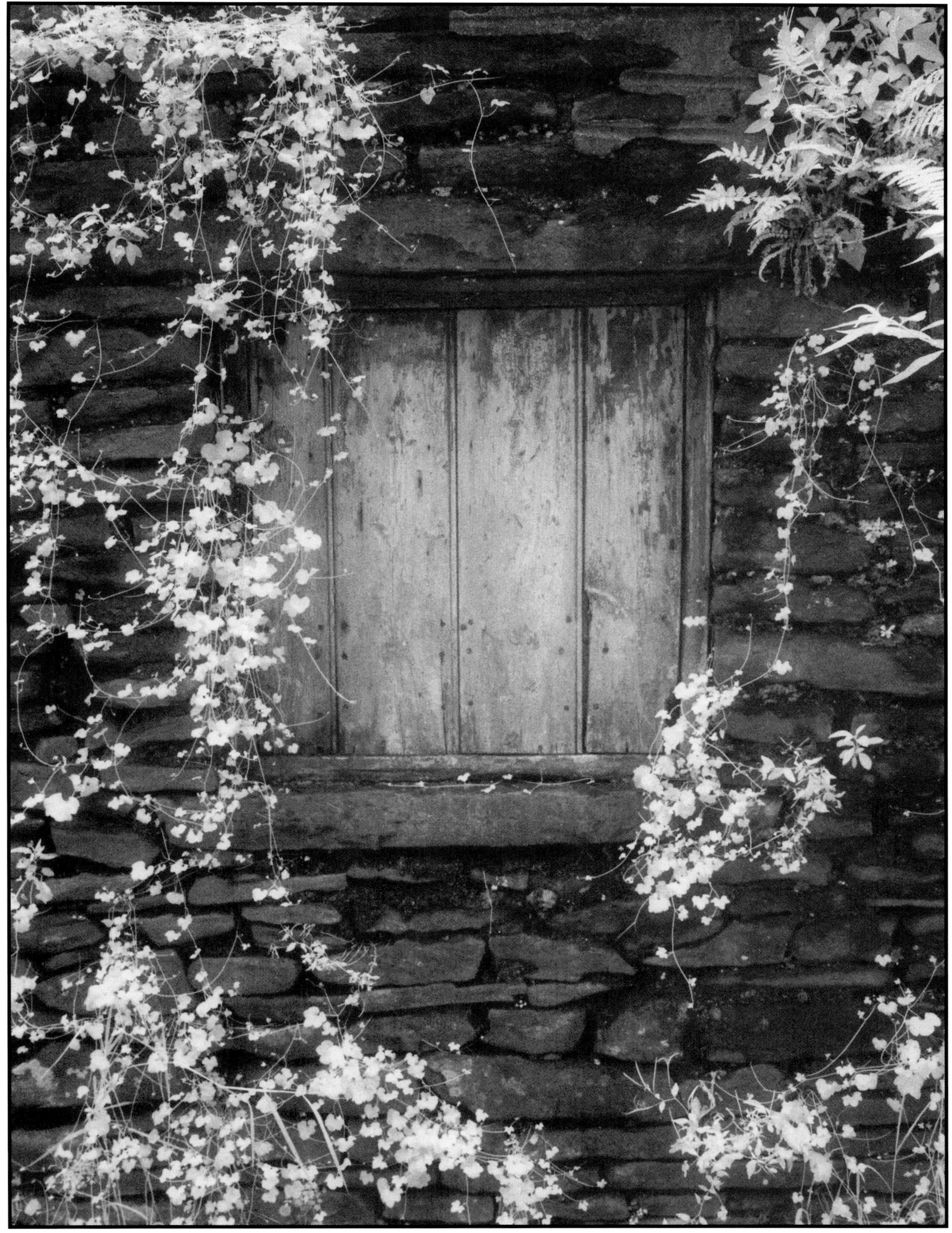

Cascade

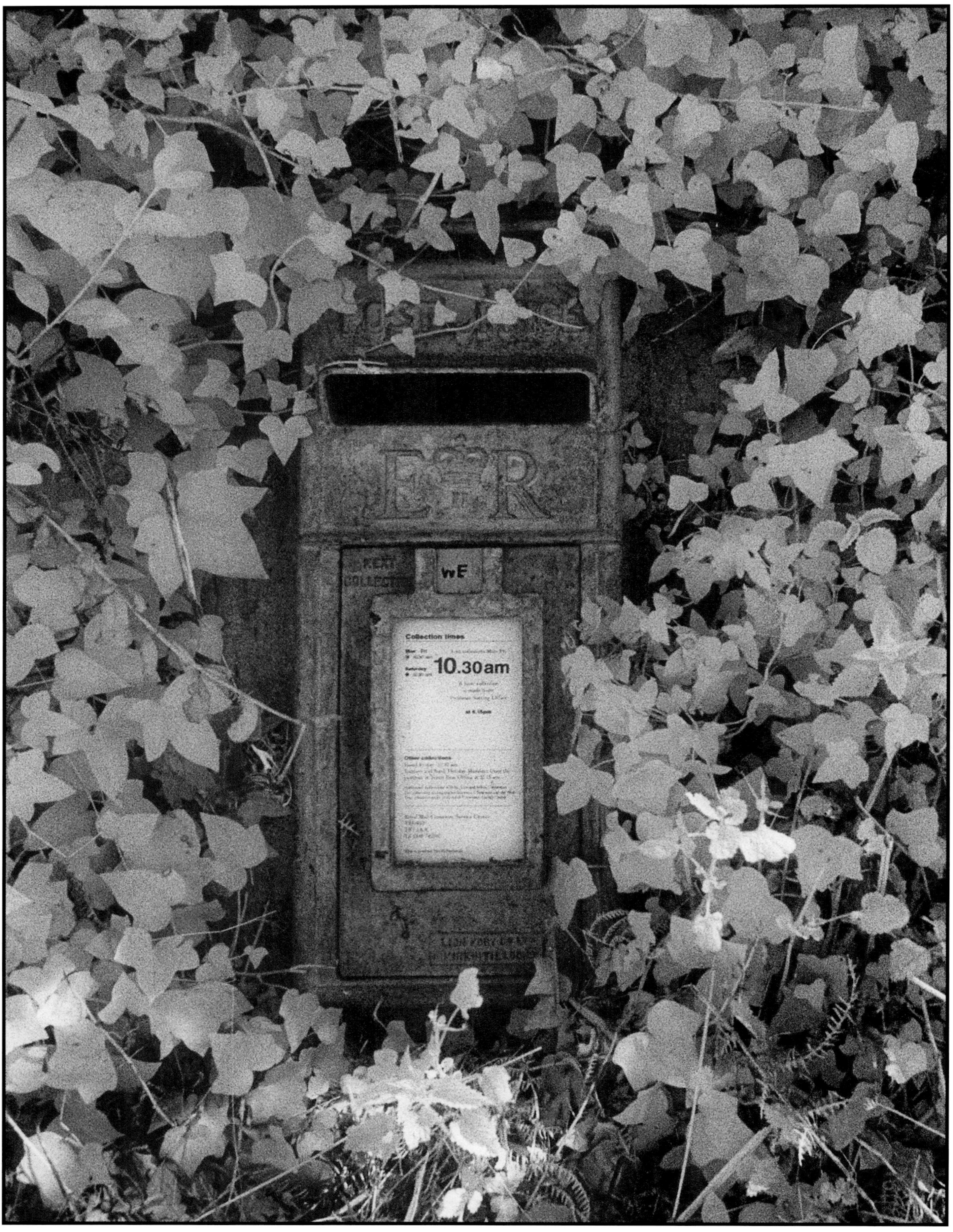
wE
Collection times
10.30am

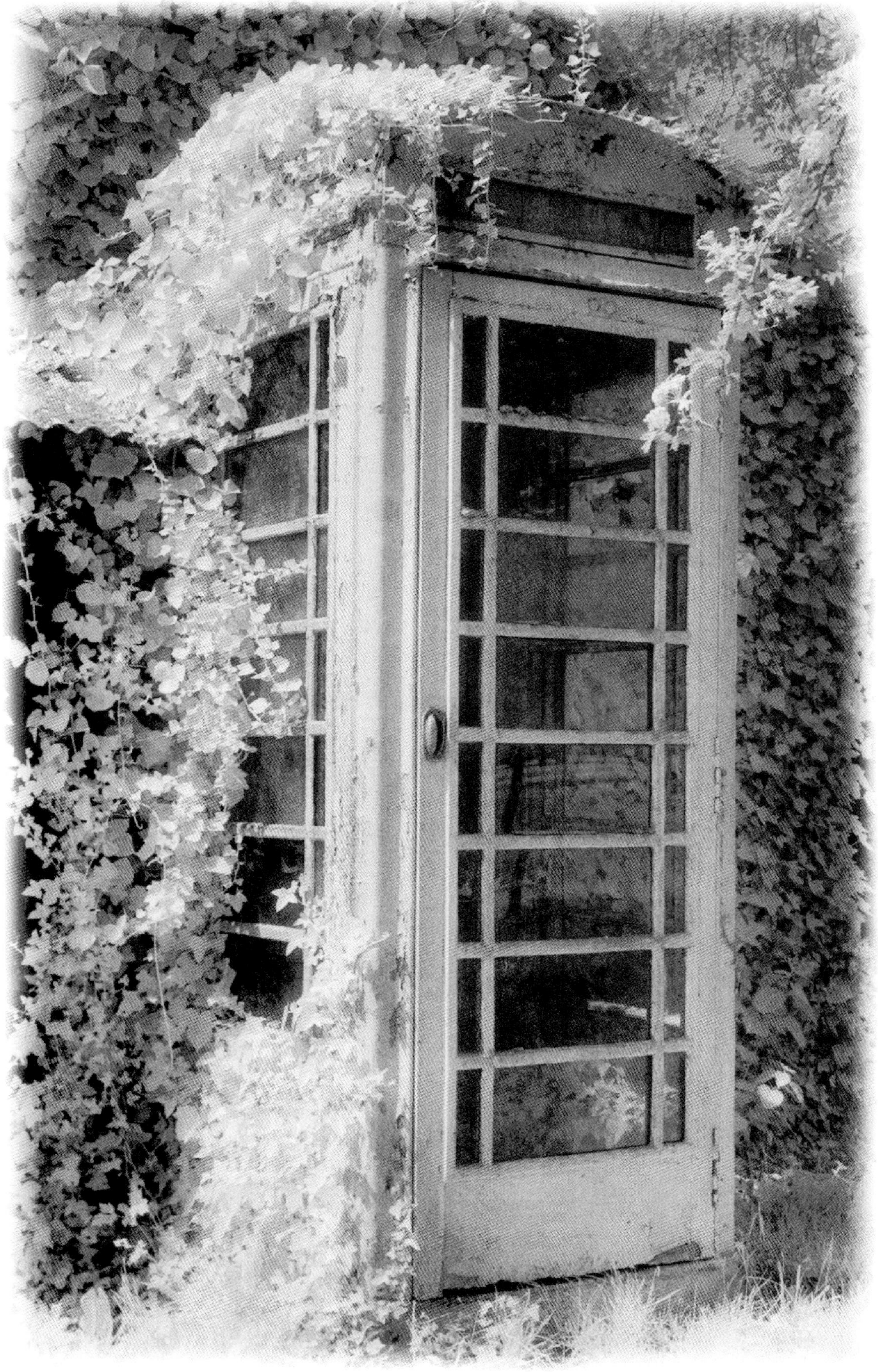

(left)
10.30 post

(right)
Telephone box

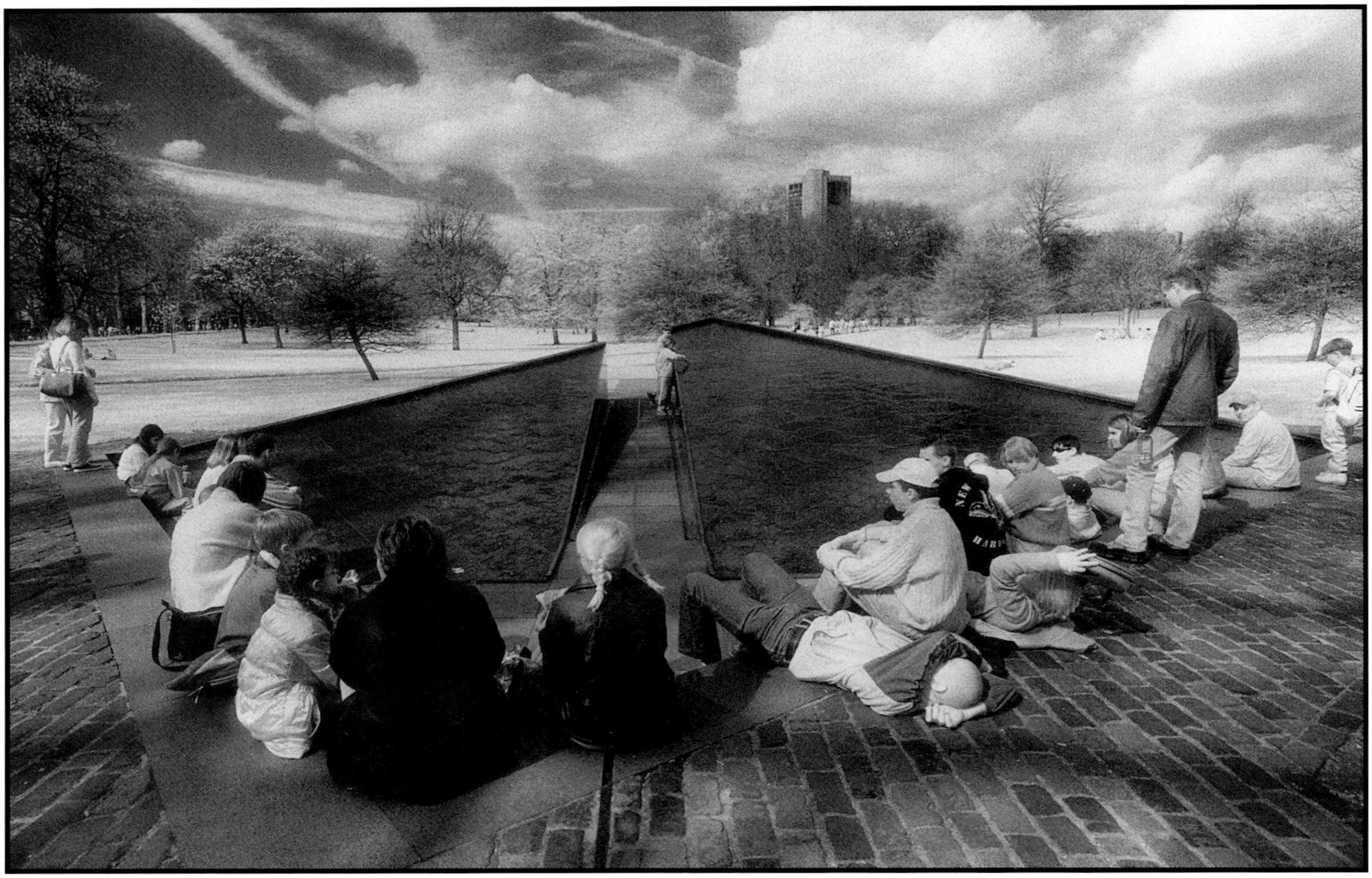

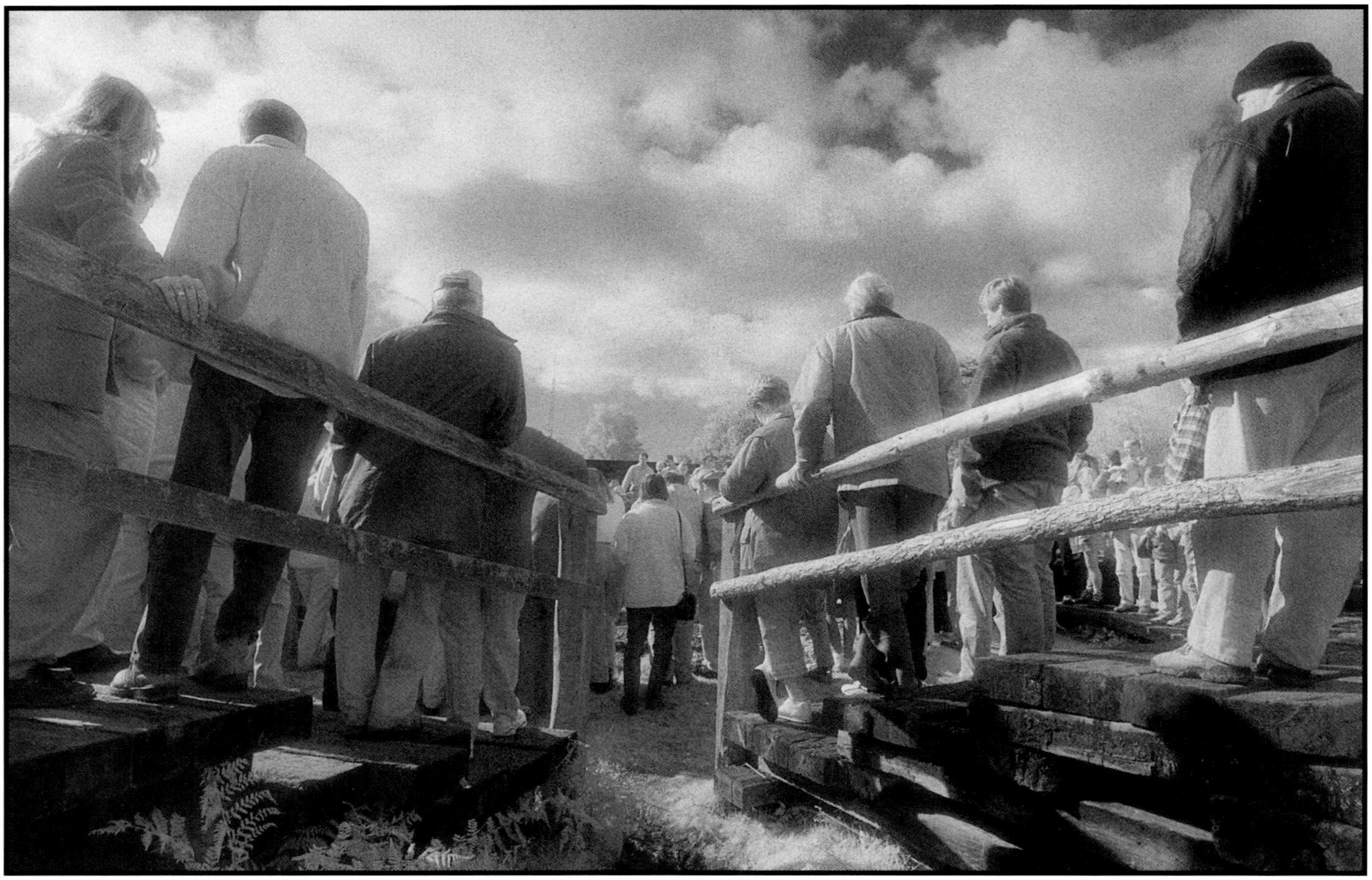

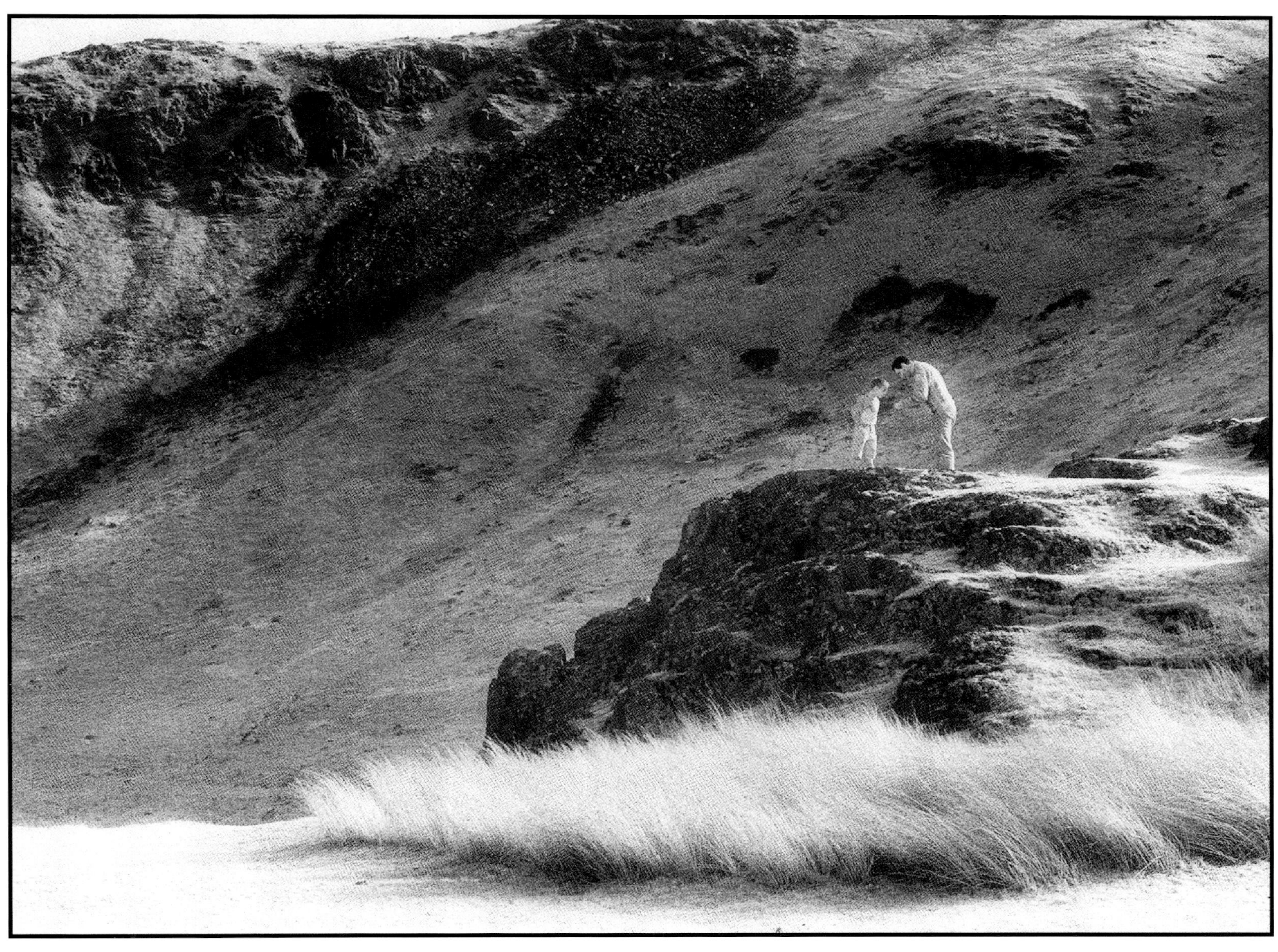

(above)
Father and son

(top left)
Day out

(bottom left)
Spectators

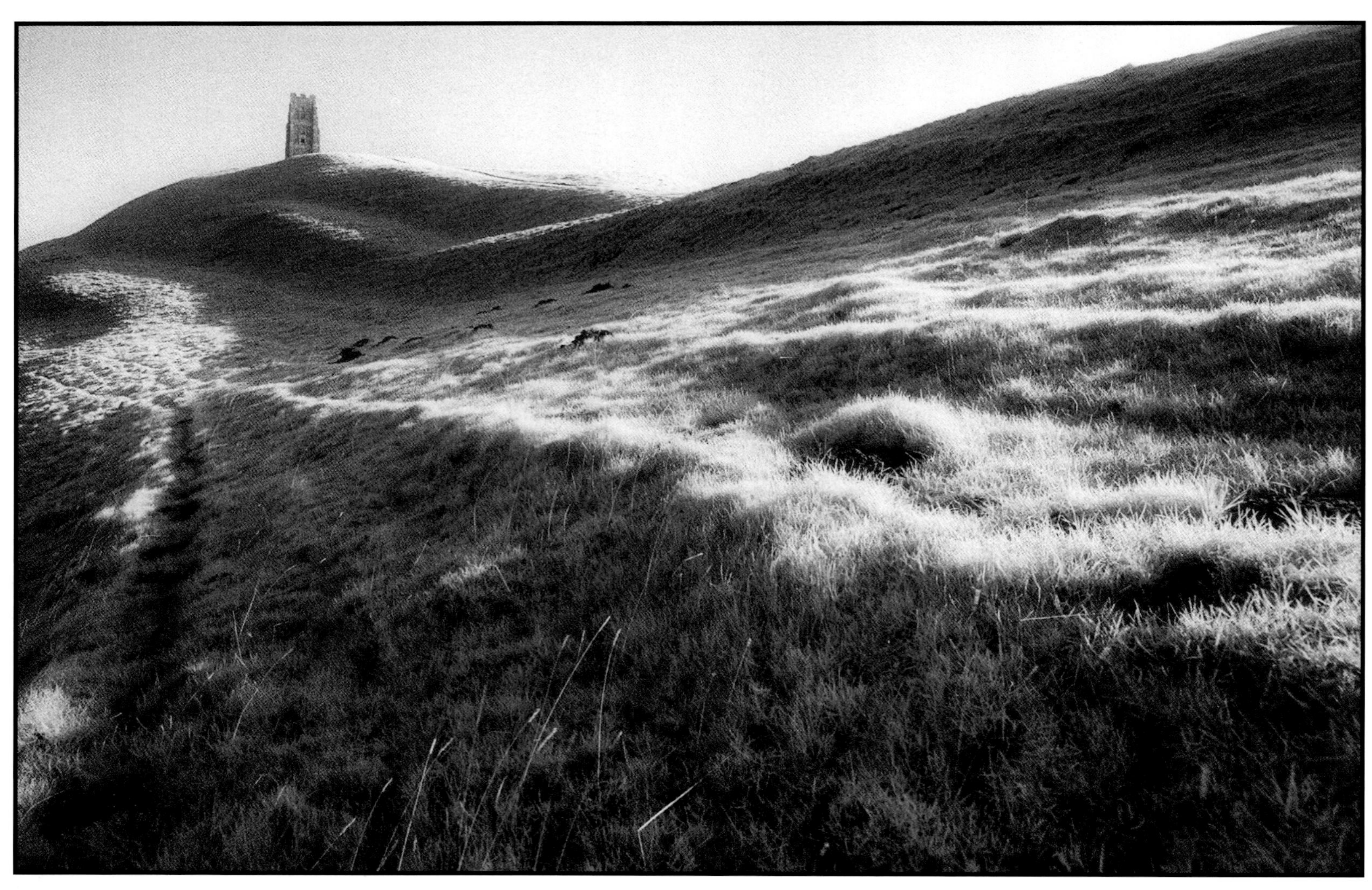

(above)
Glastonbury Tor

(top right)
Glastonbury Abbey

(bottom right)
Lakeland fells

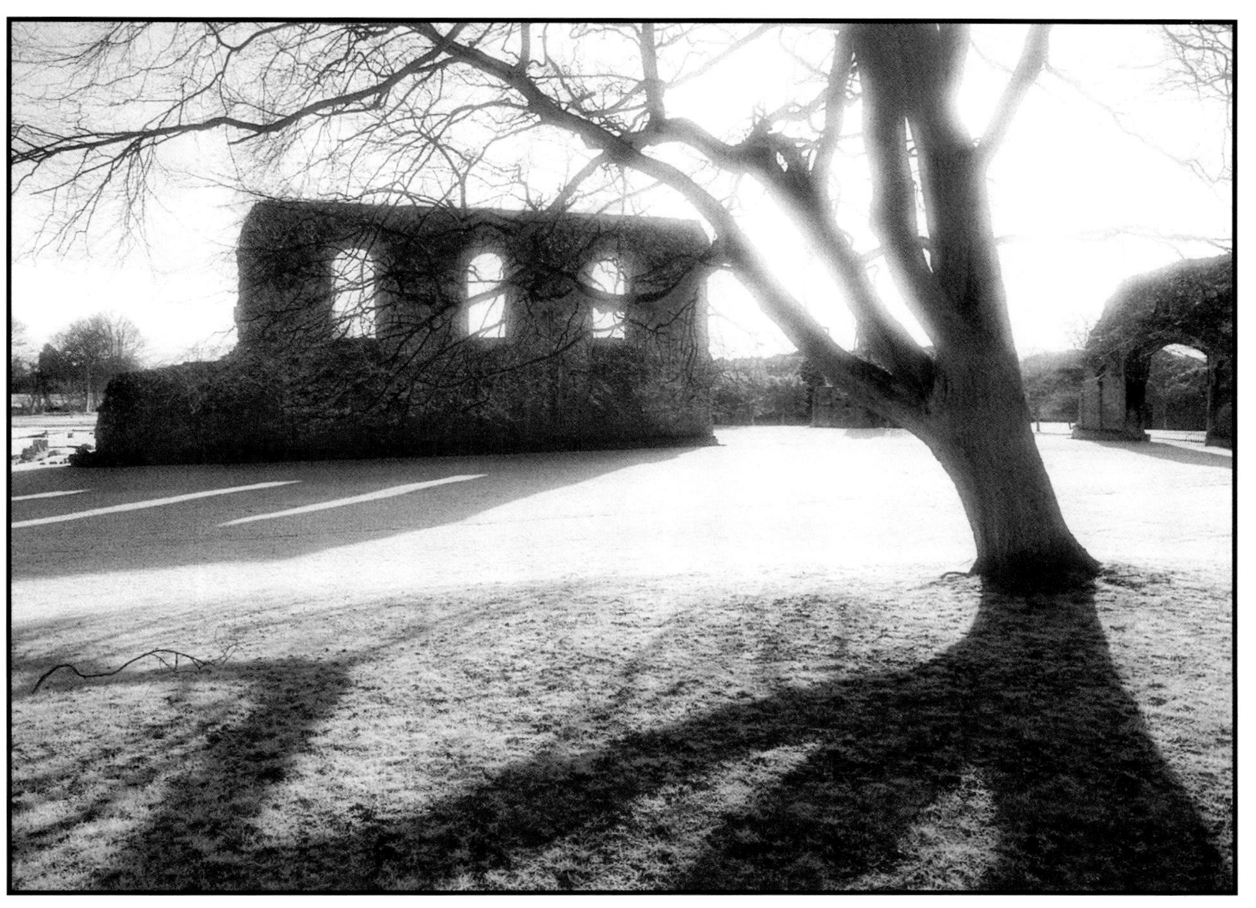

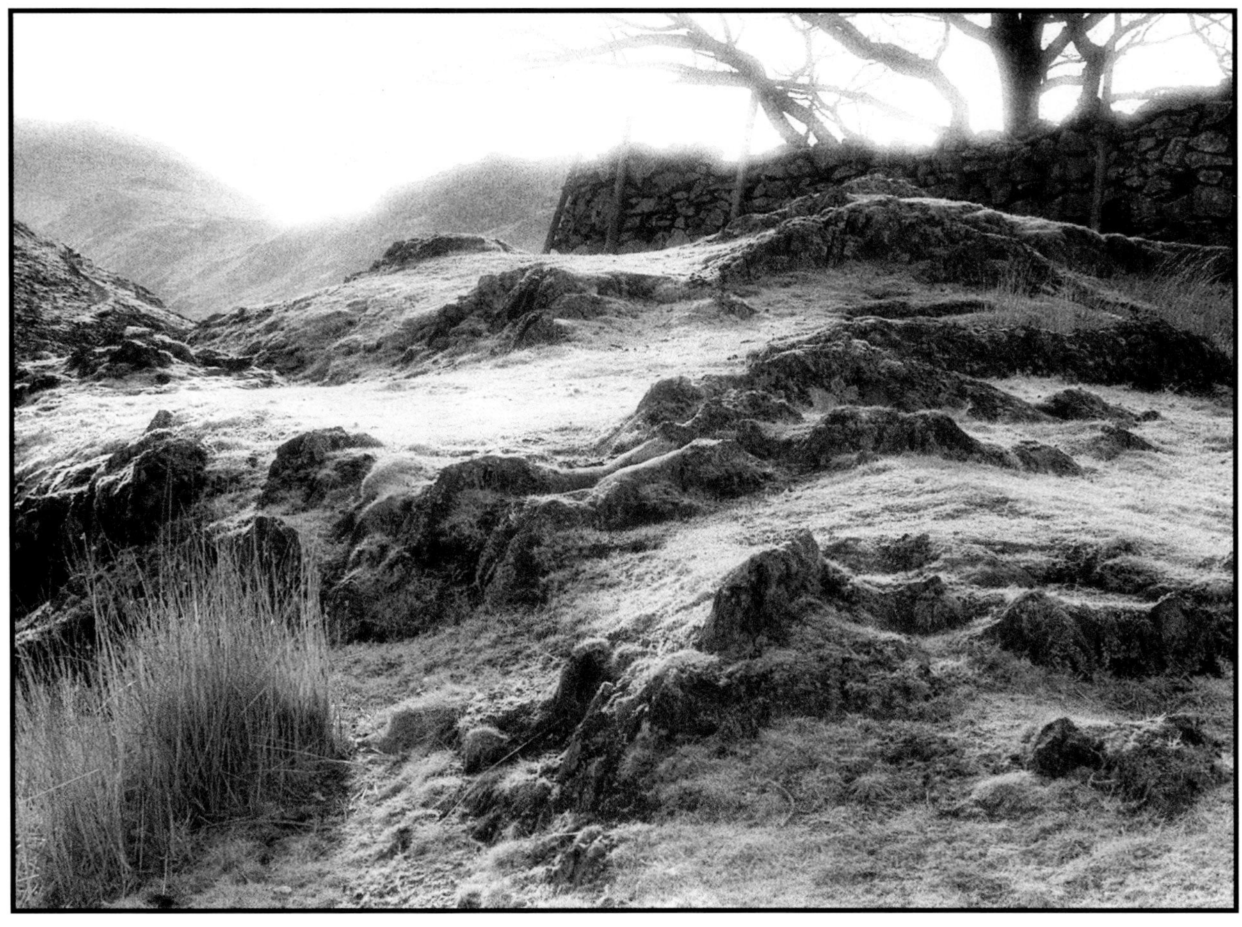

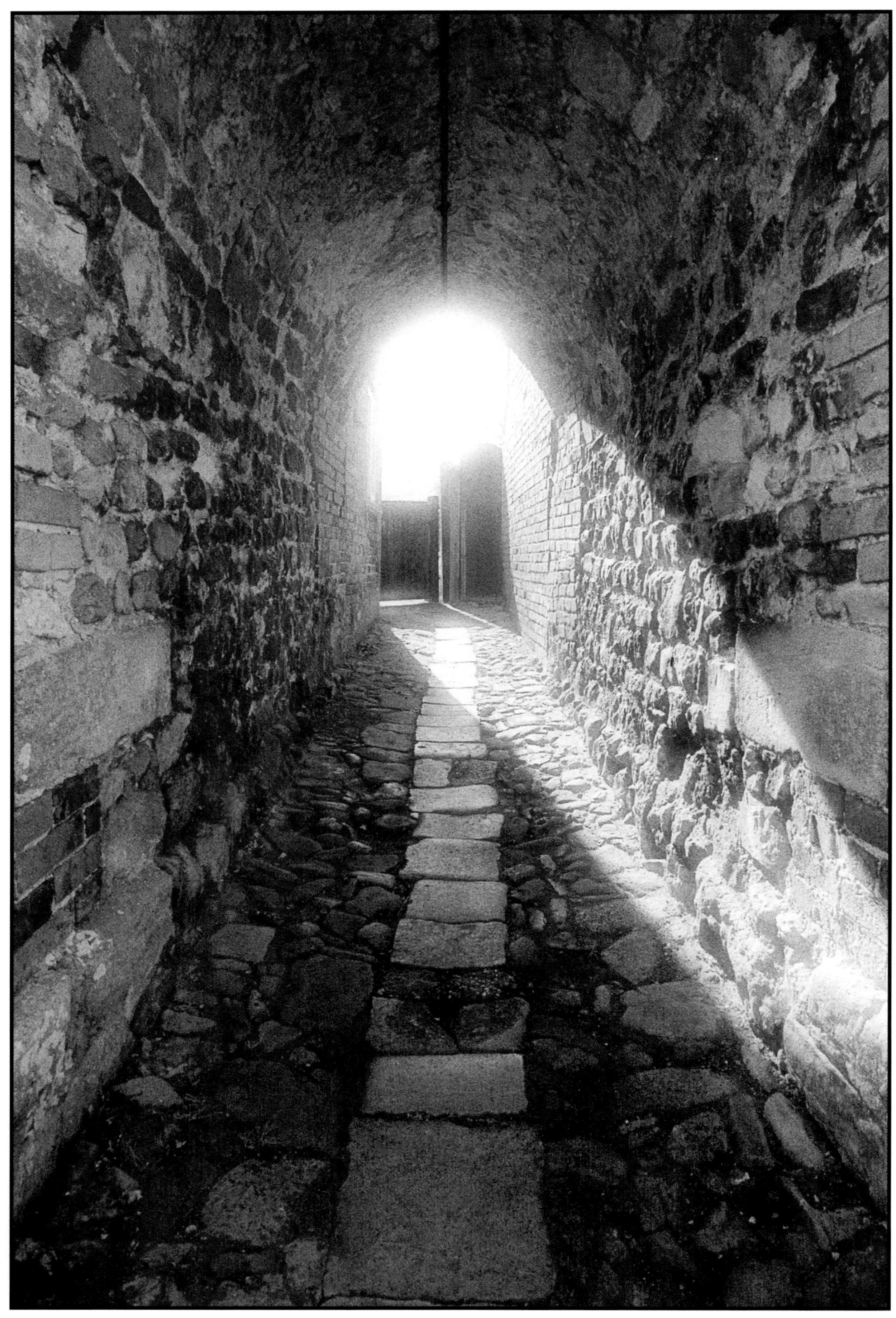

(left)
Passage to the gates

(right)
Steps

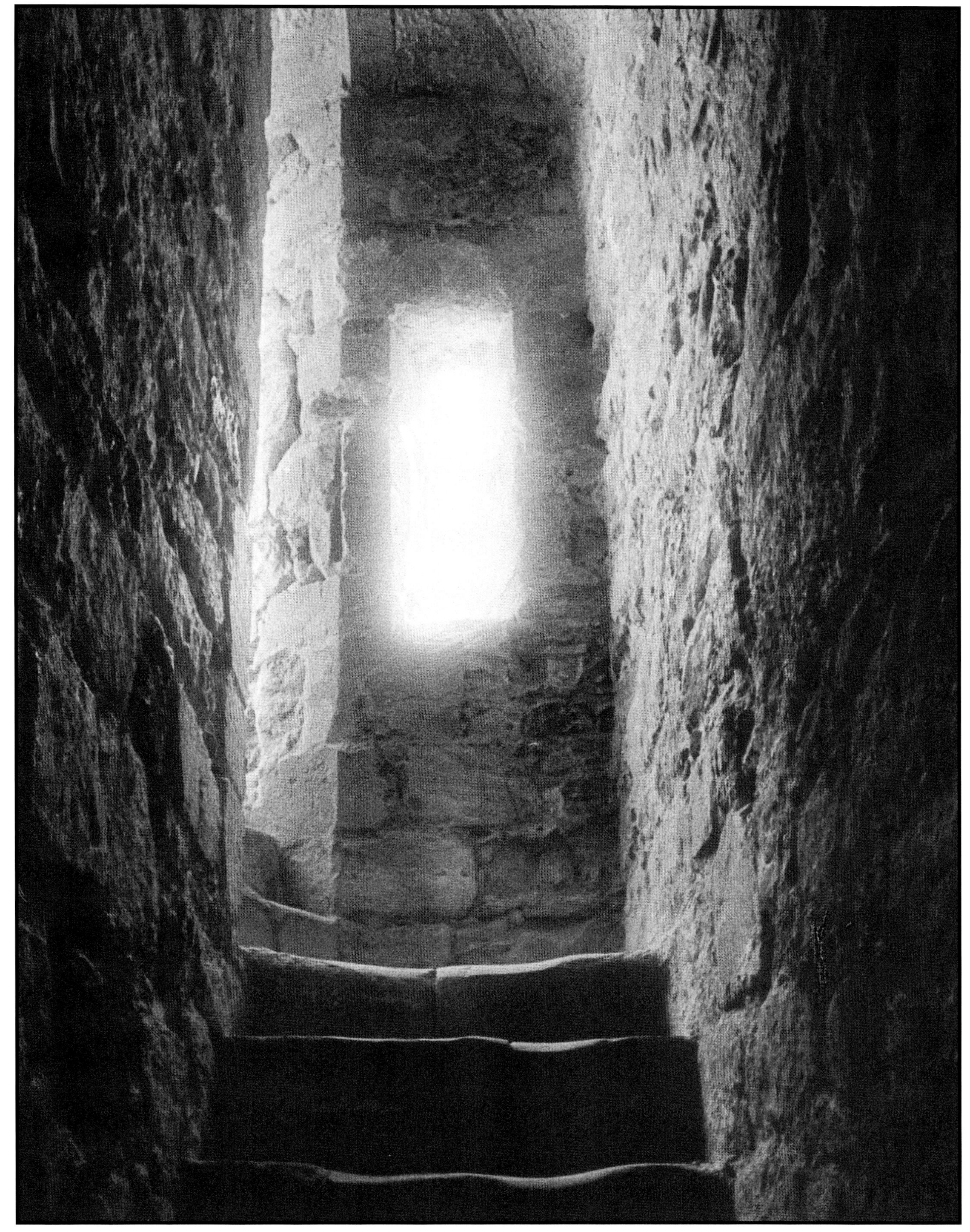

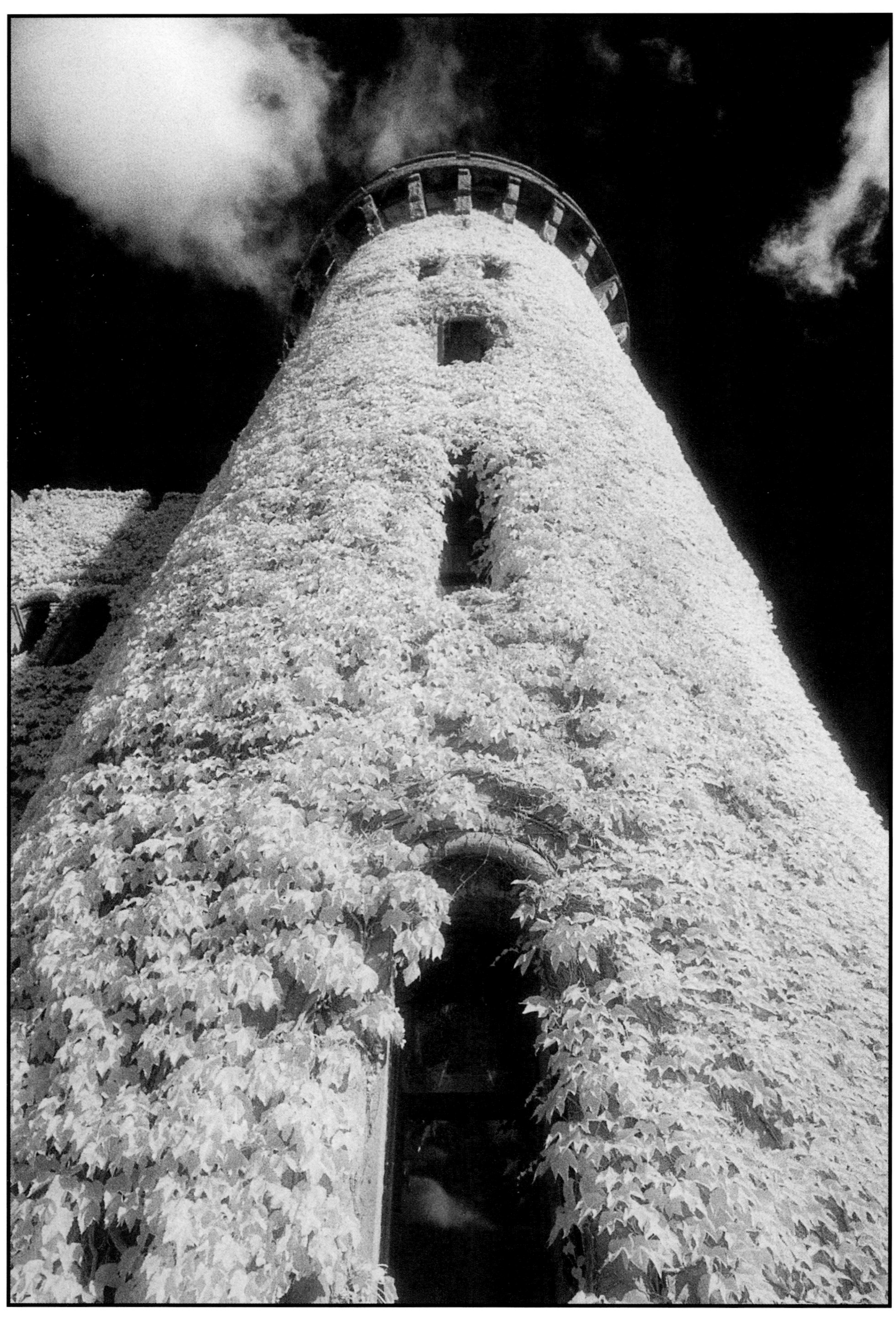

Castle Tower

HAND-COLOURING INTRODUCTION

The artistry and craft involved in making my own prints has always been intrinsic to my personal fulfilment in image making. My interest in handcolouring was perhaps a natural progression. Portrayal of mood and atmosphere, and even emphasis, become more readily controllable with careful selection of colour, tone and hue. I feel this very personal expression of colour and communication gives handtinted pictures a charm and uniqueness that can set them apart from other photographs.

COLOURING MATERIALS

The handcolouring materials I like to use are Marshall's Photo Oils and Pencils, or Photo Dyes when these are more suited to my picture. These translucent materials allow the photographic image, including subtle details and tones, to be seen through the colour layers.

Generally, choice of paper is determined by its suitability to subject and the colouring materials used. Things to consider include the base tone, the surface texture and whether the paper is resin-coated or fibre-based.

Resin coated papers readily accept dyes, but they are not suited to oils which rely on the paper having a 'tooth' to allow them to adhere. If you particularly want to use a smooth surface paper, you can apply a Pre-Colour spay which puts a skin across the surface of the print allowing the oils to grip.

Although harder to handle, I feel the fibre papers are an excellent choice for handcolouring. The most receptive surfaces are 'matt' and art/textured.

For oils and pencils, my favourite paper is Kentmere's Art Classic. This is a fibre-based, heavyweight and warm tone paper with a lovely ivory base and a beautiful tonal quality. I also like Ilford Multigrade IV FB matt and Multigrade FB Warmtone semi-matt. These papers have a smooth surface, receive oils readily and have the added benefit of being variable contrast. For dyes, my favourites are Ilford Multigrade IV FB and Warmtone, both in glossy surfaces.

PRINTING FOR HANDCOLOURING

Many subjects work well, including portraits, landscapes, still life and texture studies. Above all, it is important to choose an image you really 'love', as the process of colouring can be lengthy.

Prints that tend to accept colours easily are those containing a fair amount of light and highlight tones and of average contrast. Stark black areas are difficult, as the colour tends to sit on top of absolute black.

When colouring a whole picture, I find it best to make my print slightly lighter than usual. If colouring only a portion of the picture I do not alter the overall density, I just dodge the chosen area a little.

Prints may be toned prior to handcolouring, but it is not essential. In many ways, the 'black and white' underlying images give the picture its distinctive 'handcrafted' look. However, there may be times when you want the background tone to be modified to suit the subject. Sepia gives added warmth to the base print and is especially good in portraiture or in pictures rich in yellows and browns. Seascapes and atmospheric landscapes can benefit from a cool blue underlying hue, available with the use of blue or gold. Selenium, sepia and gold toners also have the added benefit of assisting with archival permanence of fibre prints.

OILS AND PENCILS

Marshall's oils and pencils are gorgeous for handcolouring. Oils are acid free, permanent and come in a range of over 50 colours. Most of these are standard strength and some in stronger variants. From these a vast range of colours can be mixed, ranging from subtle muted tints to intense and vibrant colours. They are sold either as individual tubes or in sets of varying sizes together with ancillary products to aid application. They are expensive to buy, but you only need to use a small amount to colour each picture, so they last a long time. There is also a range of nearly 30 pencils, which can either be used on their own to colour images or to complement the oils.

They are easy and enjoyable to use and very forgiving. Nothing needs to be final until you want it that way. Before they dry, the oils can be changed, lightened or darkened, or partially or totally removed. This makes correction of mistakes and re-application easy and painless.

Apart from the oils and pencils you will need:

Extender: Mixed with oils, this substance will make colours paler without thinning. It is also useful for cleaning small areas.
Prepared Medium (PM) Solution: Used on rough papers as a pre-coating solution, before application of oils and pencils. It can also be used for cleaning.
Marlene: A cleaner for removing dyes from the entire print or palette.
Extras to help: 100% cotton wool balls, cotton buds, wrapped tooth-picks, and brushes, vinyl eraser, canned air, low tack tape, palette, colour wheel, thick card to hold your print steady, and good light to work in.

APPLICATION OF THE OILS

I use a range of items to apply the oils including brushes, wrapped toothpicks and cotton wool balls – ready-made cotton buds are good if their size is right. Wrapping toothpicks in cotton wool provides the flexibility to make the application point large or small depending on the area you on working on. To do this: break off a piece of cotton wool the size you need and wrap this tightly around the pointed end of a damp-ened toothpick using a twisting motion. Ensure the point is covered to avoid scratching your print.

Step by step guide to colouring a whole picture:

1. Secure your print on a thick piece of card. Cover and protect the print borders with low tack removable tape.
2. Choose the colour mixes you want to use and test these on discarded prints. A colour wheel can be a useful aid. If using a colour mix ensure you make sufficient to complete the whole area you want to

HAND-COLOURING INTRODUCTION

colour – it may be difficult to mix the exact colour again. Oils can be used straight from the tube or dispensed on palette and picked up from there.

3. The first colouring stage involves making a swift and rough application of colour across the whole print. Don't worry about going outside lines, causing overruns or covering over small details at this point. As you change from one colour to the next, gently rub down the colour you have applied with a cotton wad: this will remove any excess oil and even out the colour. Work your way around the picture repeating this process until all the main colour areas are covered.
4. Once this general wash is complete, go back and introduce colour into the smaller areas. When applying a new colour, this one takes precedence, and will lift the one beneath, clearing up overruns and allowing you to add and alter colours. (Caution: applying yellow to a blue overrun should be avoided as a green colour cast can occur.)
5. In the next stage, add tone and detail to the shadow areas and colour and clean up highlight areas: this will begin to shape and put form into the picture. Change the cotton wool regularly when cleaning up areas and use canned air to remove accumulated dust particles from the print.
6. The final colouring stage is to go over the print adding very fine details, using pencils, small applicators and brushes. These little details define your particularly important areas and bring the picture to life.
7. To finish carefully check there are no areas of excess oil remaining on the print. If there are removed these gently with cotton wool wads. Remove your print from the backing board; clean up overruns in the border area and leave to dry.
8. Proper drying can take anywhere from 3 to 10 days depending on the drying environment and quantity of oil paint used. Drying can be speeded if necessary by using a solution of 'Drier' another Marshall's product.

DYES

I often use dyes when I am colouring only selected areas within a print, or when I want to use a glossy paper. Concentrated dyes are available in sets that can be diluted and mixed to make a wide variety of colours. The dyes can be used on a range of photographic surfaces, are inexpensive to buy and last a long time. Unlike oils, which dry on to the paper surface, dyes are completely absorbed by the emulsion. They also adhere almost immediately upon application and so, unfortunately, if a mistake is made there is little hope of rectifying it. The only chance is to use a reducer or re-wash the paper thoroughly (though this may not be totally successful).

Other basic supplies needed include sable brushes, cotton wool wads, paper towels, mixing tray, water, wetting agent, card and removable tape. A colour wheel is also useful to aid colour choice.

APPLICATION OF DYES

Apply to small areas using very small sable brushes; for larger areas use larger brushes or cotton wool wads of appropriate sizes.

Steps to hand colouring selective areas in your picture with dyes:

1. Secure print to think piece of card, to keep it flat. Cover and protect borders.
2. Colours are very strong and need to be diluted with water. Experiment with discarded prints to check your colour choices and allow colours to dry before making a final selection. (Dyes are often intense and when wet they can be deceptive, looking much lighter than their actual dry colour).
3. When ready to start colouring, wipe over the print with a solution of wetting agent, removing any excess. This light covering will prevent the paper soaking up the dye too quickly, and will tend to soften the edges of the dyes as they are applied giving a more realistic result.
4. Now you can add your colours using whichever brush or cotton wool wads you feel to be appropriate to the area you are colouring. Pick up a small amount of the colour you need, removing the excess – just check intensity by dabbing on a spare piece of paper – before applying to your print. Work from left to right if right-handed (or the opposite if you are left-handed) and work top-to-bottom to avoid any smudging.
5. Use a slow and staged approach, colours should be added gradually; lay down your first colours, then pause to allow these to dry, before moving on to build up colours and add shading. I always have a supply of pre-moistened cotton wool wads ready to keep in-check any pooling of dyes, and to wipe down larger areas; this helps to ensure even application.
6. When finished, remove from backing board and leave to dry.

Handcolouring requires time and patience and the techniques take a while to master, but is vastly rewarding. Each and every print is truly one of a kind.

(right)
Doorway

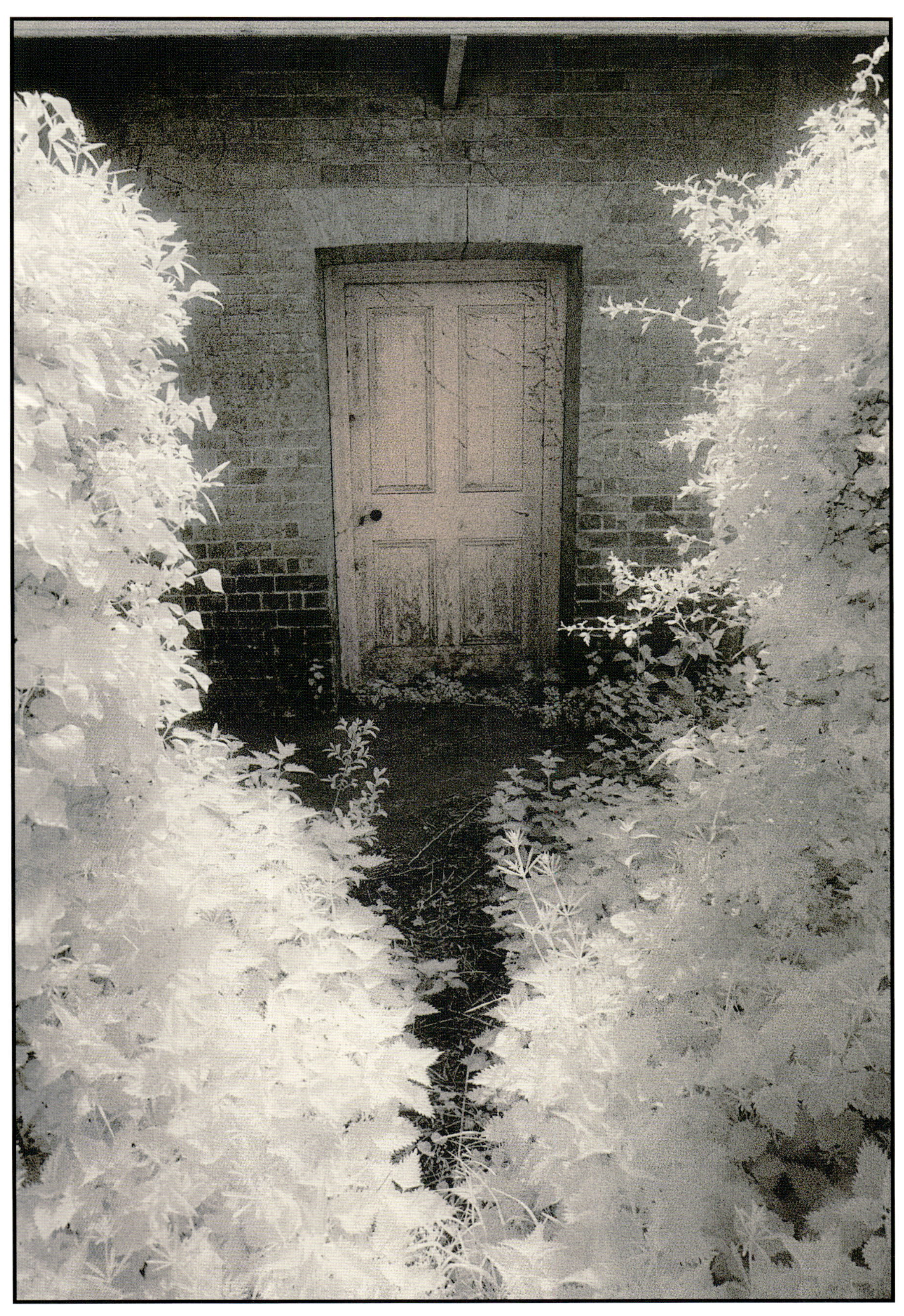

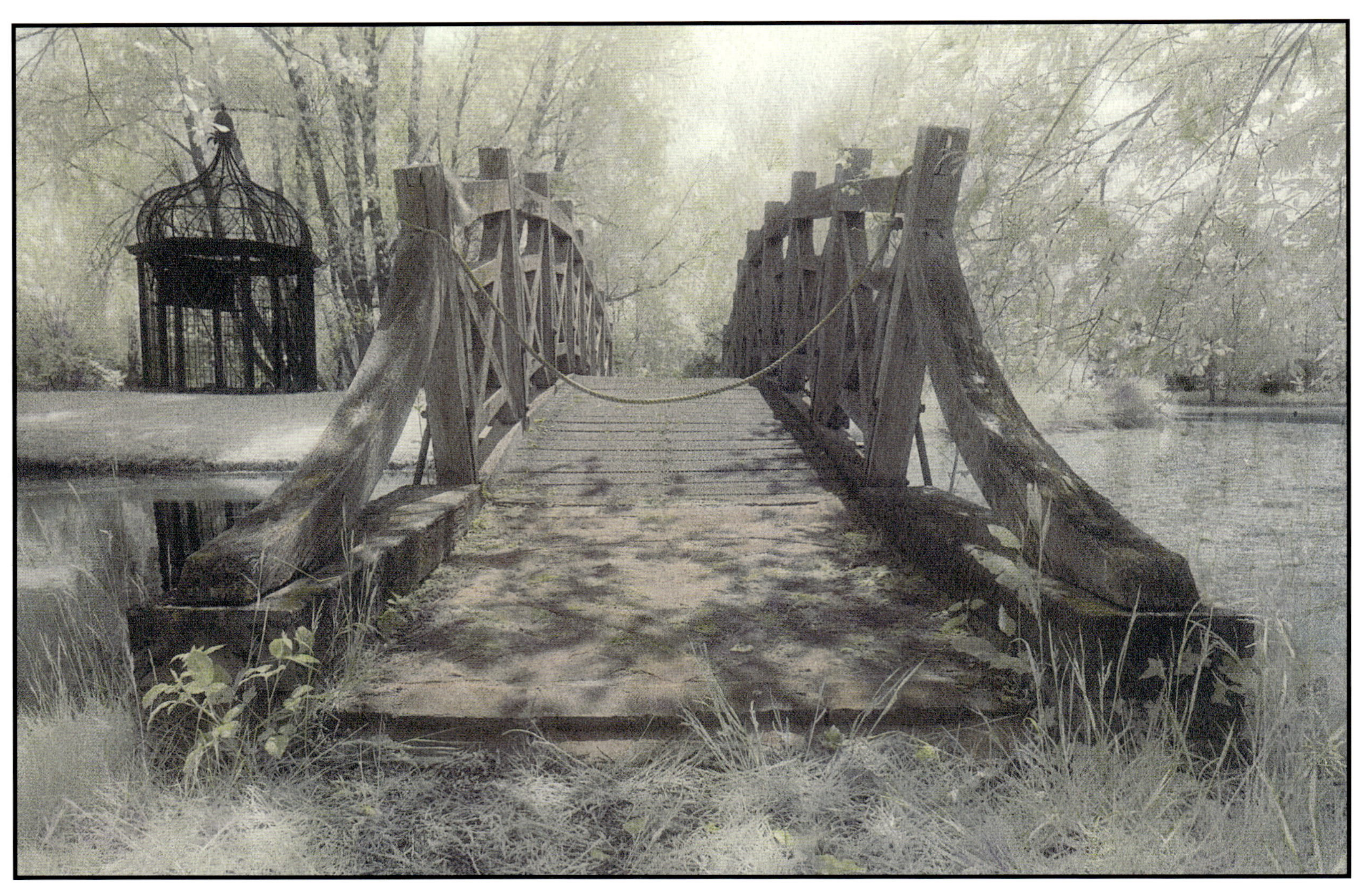

(above)
Bridge to the aviary

(top right)
The gateway

(bottom right)
Locked and forgotten

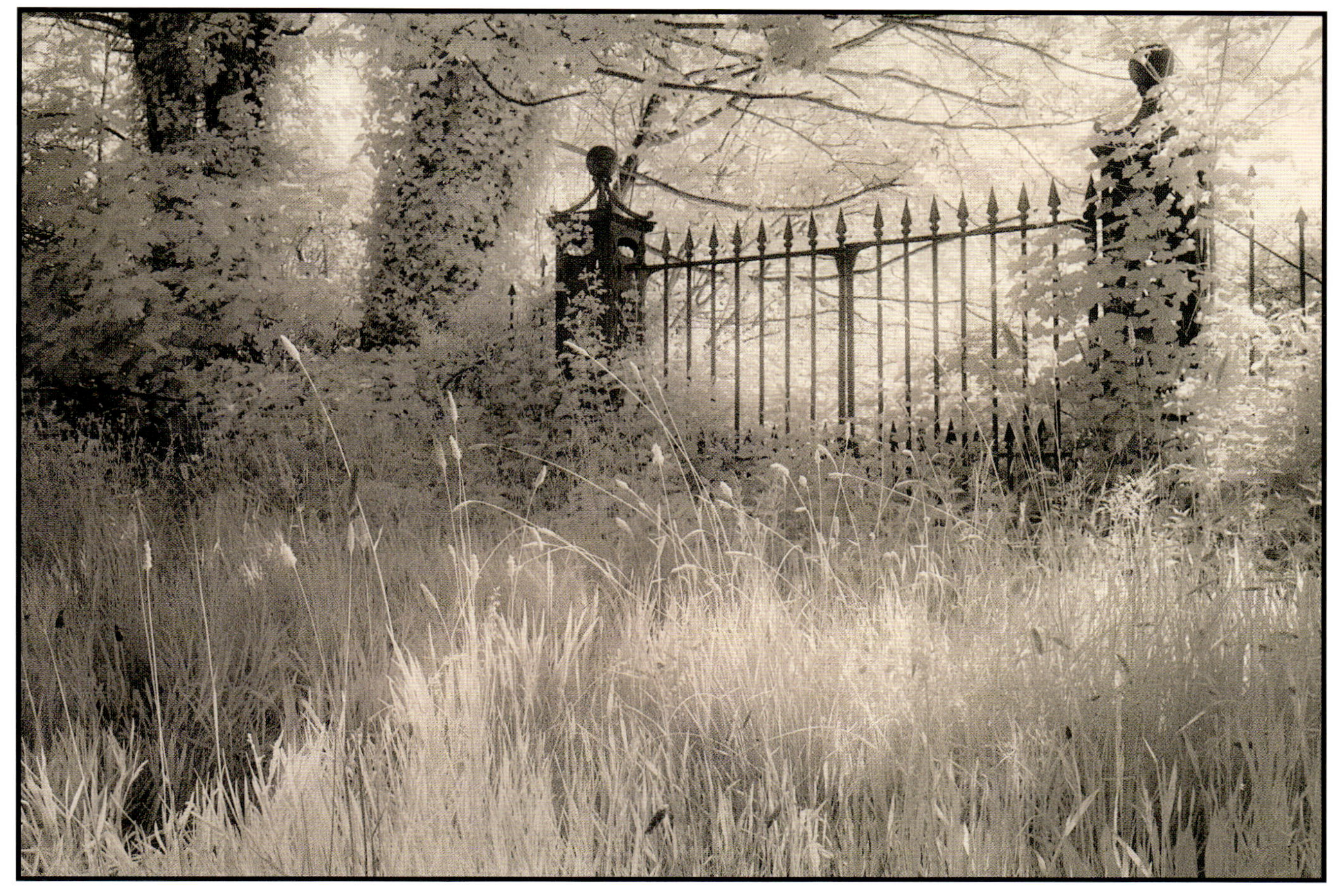

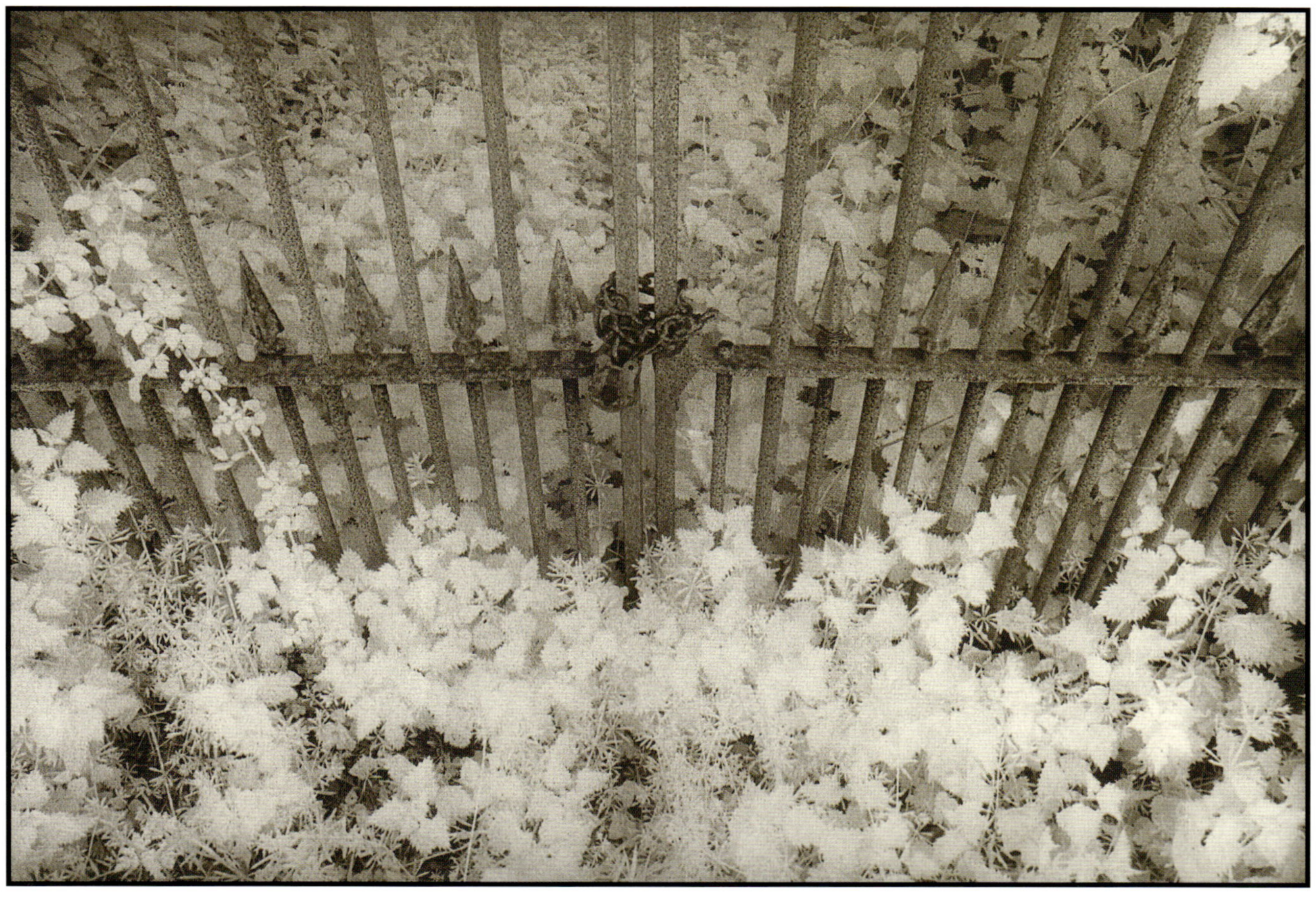

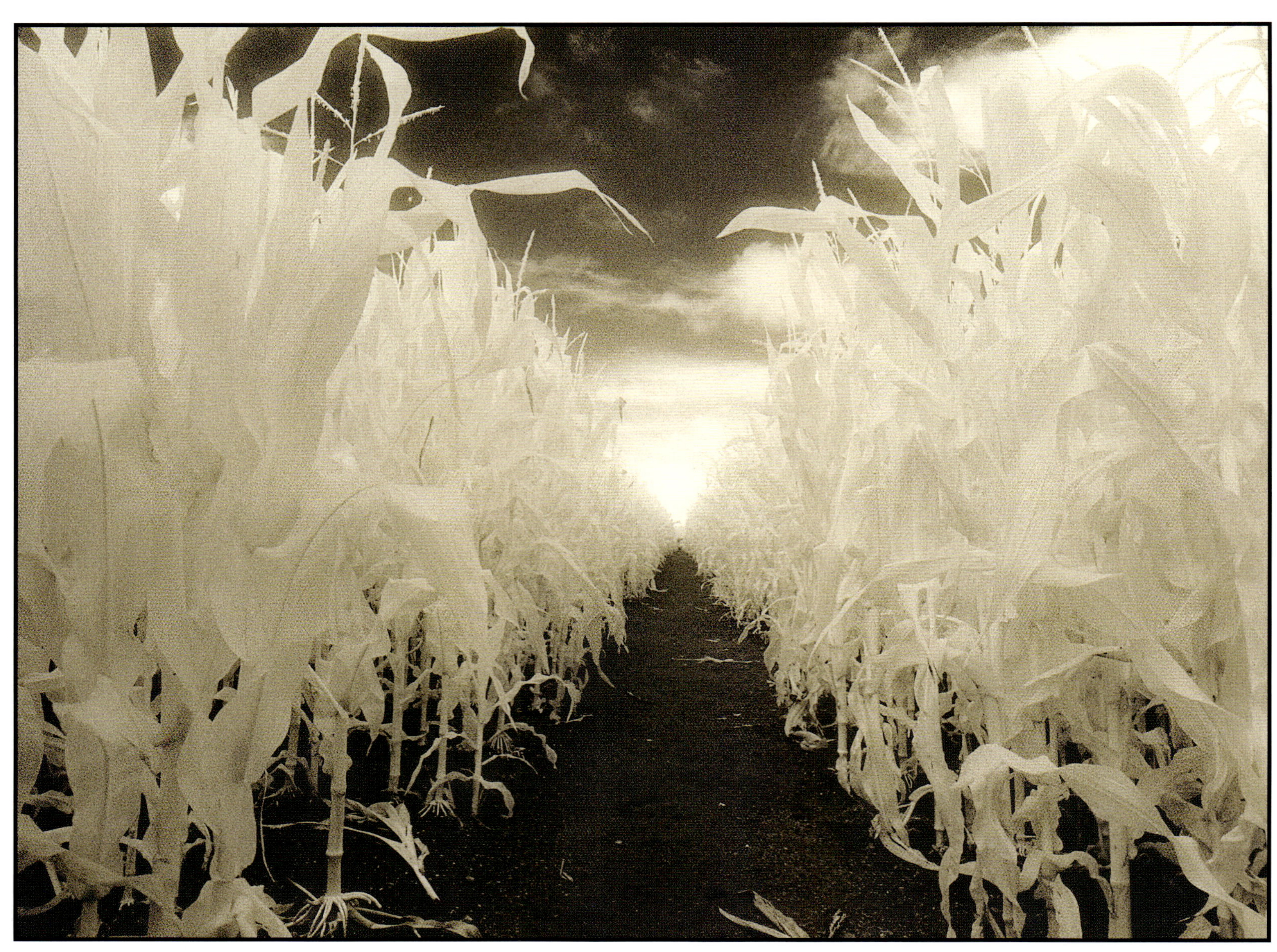

(above)
Corn field

(top right)
Garlic, shallots and potatoes #2

(bottom right)
Garlic, shallots and potatoes #1

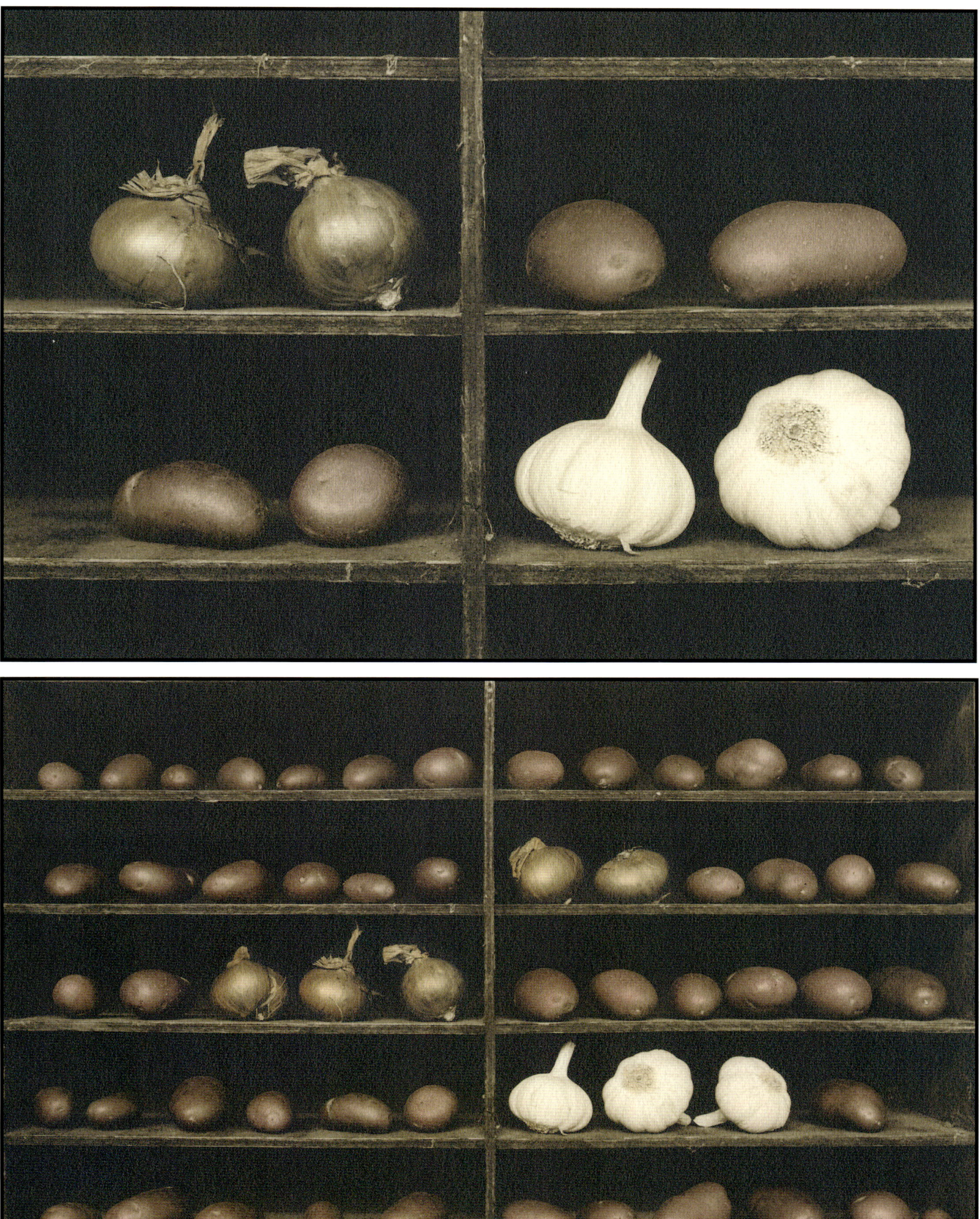

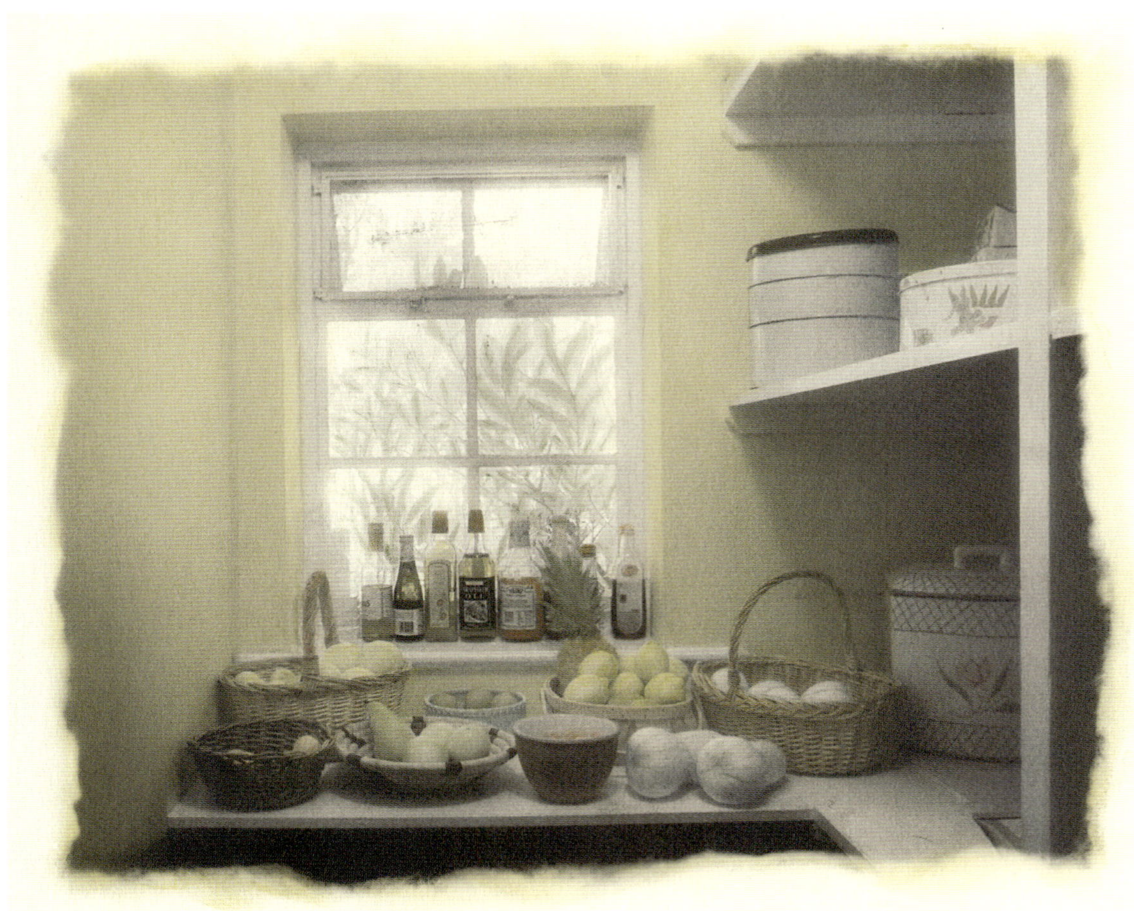

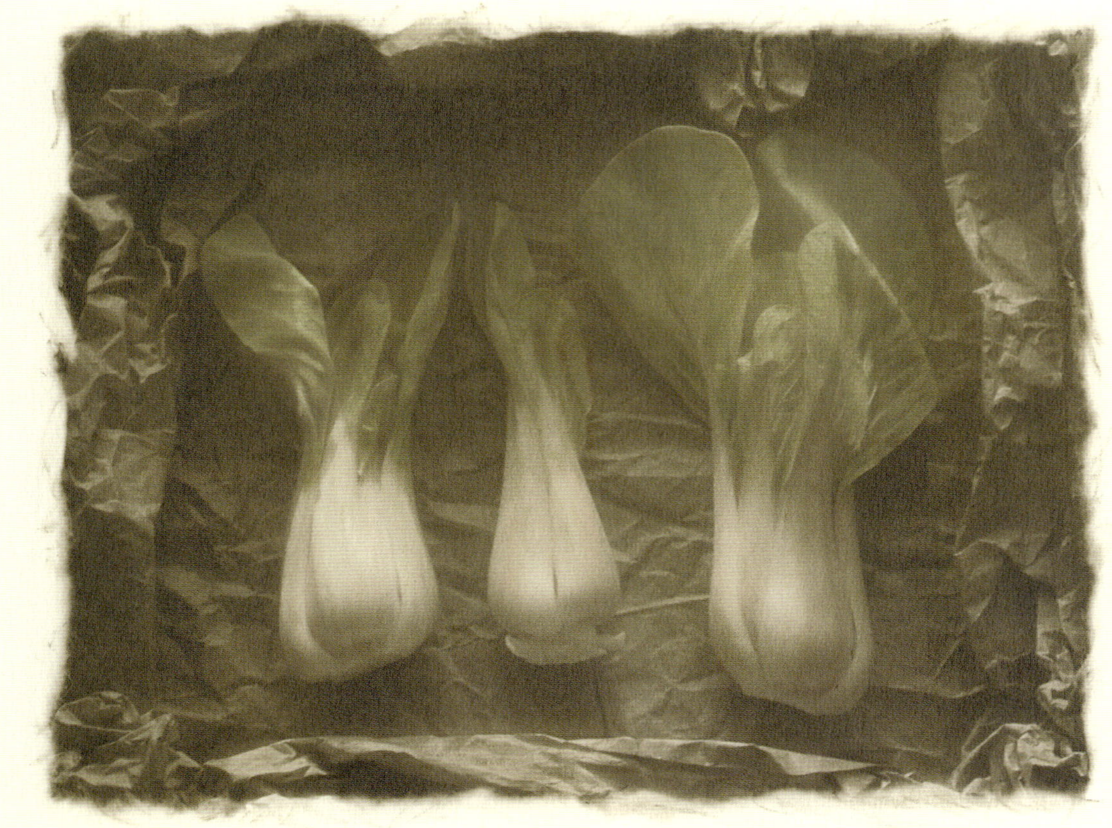

(top left)
The Pantry

(top right)
Asparagus and petal

(bottom left)
Pak Choi

(bottom right)
Pear and periwinkle

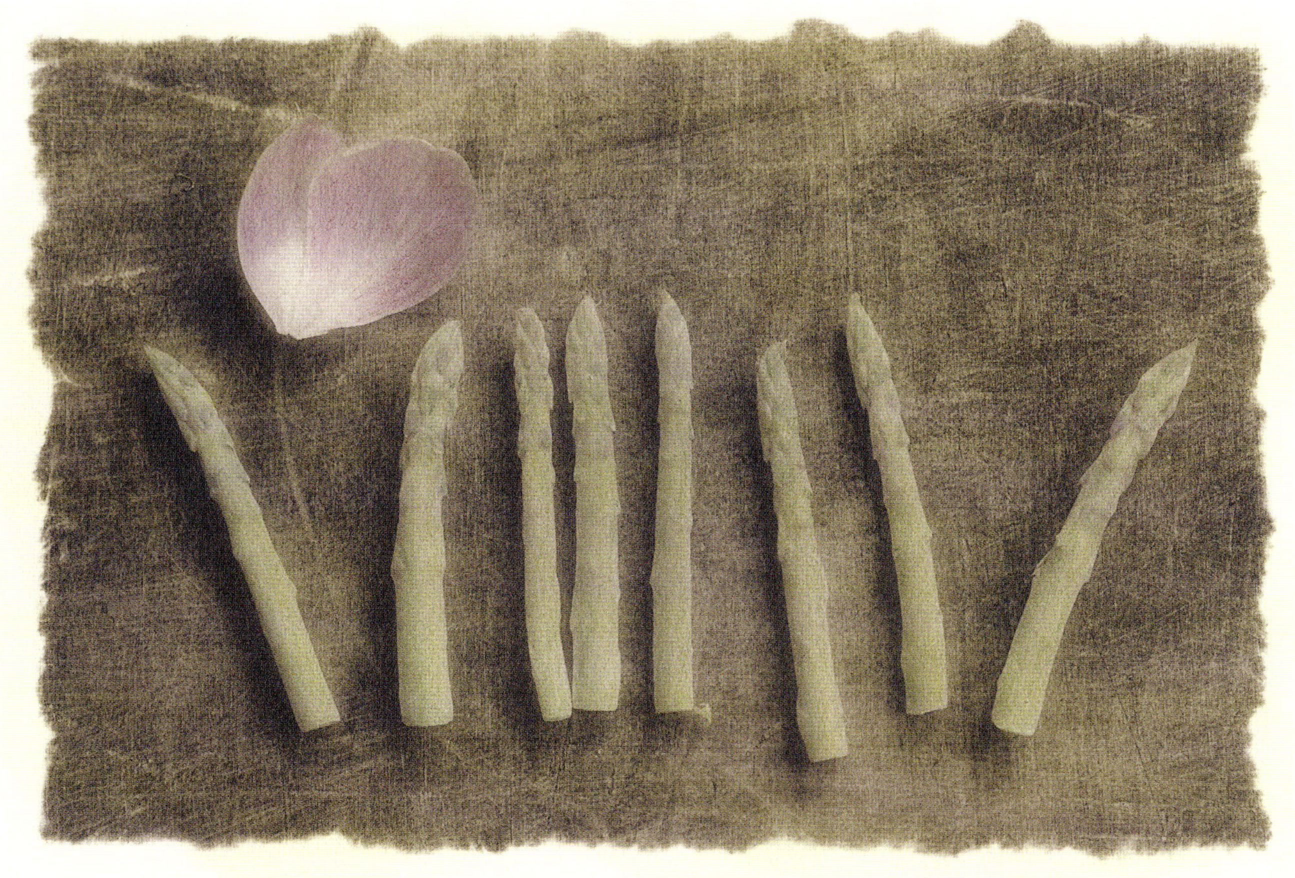

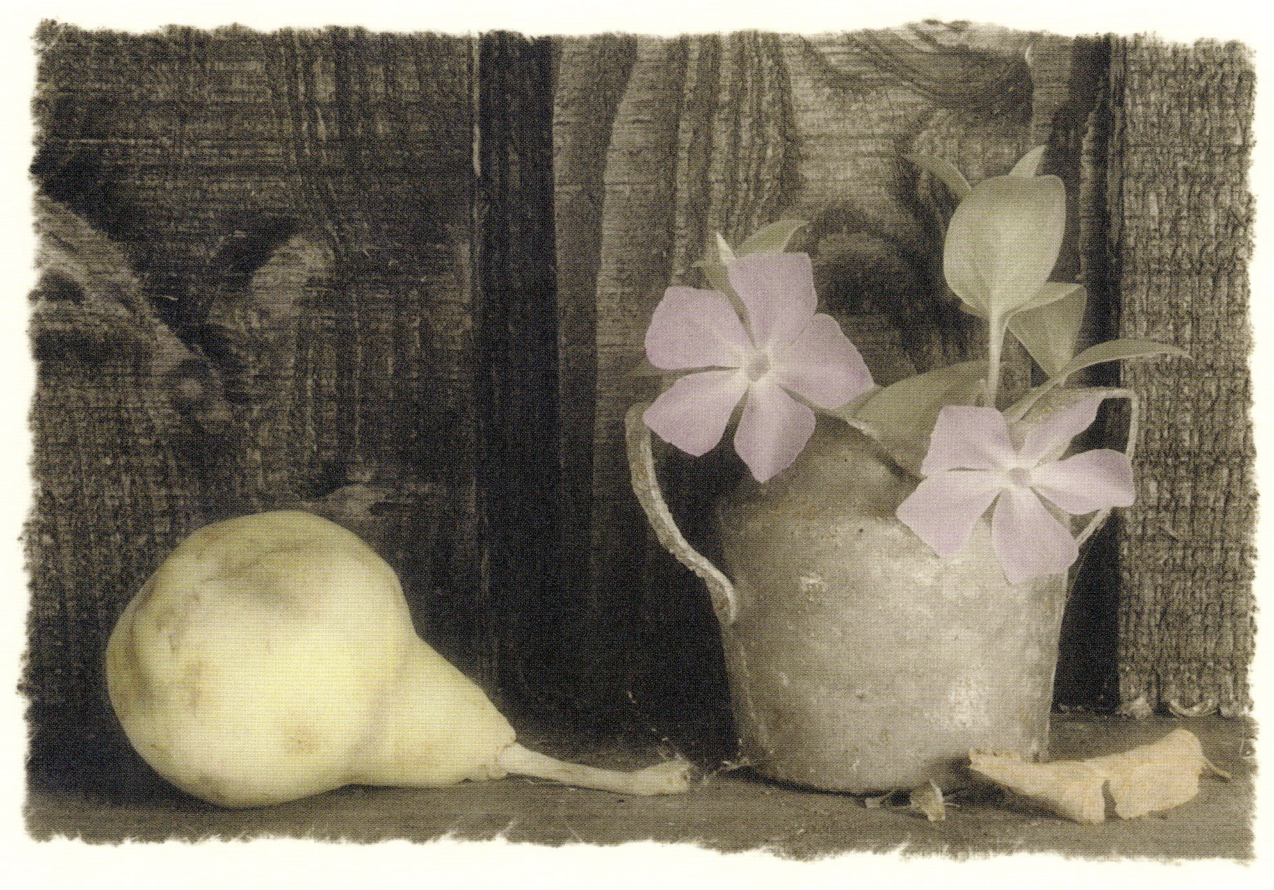

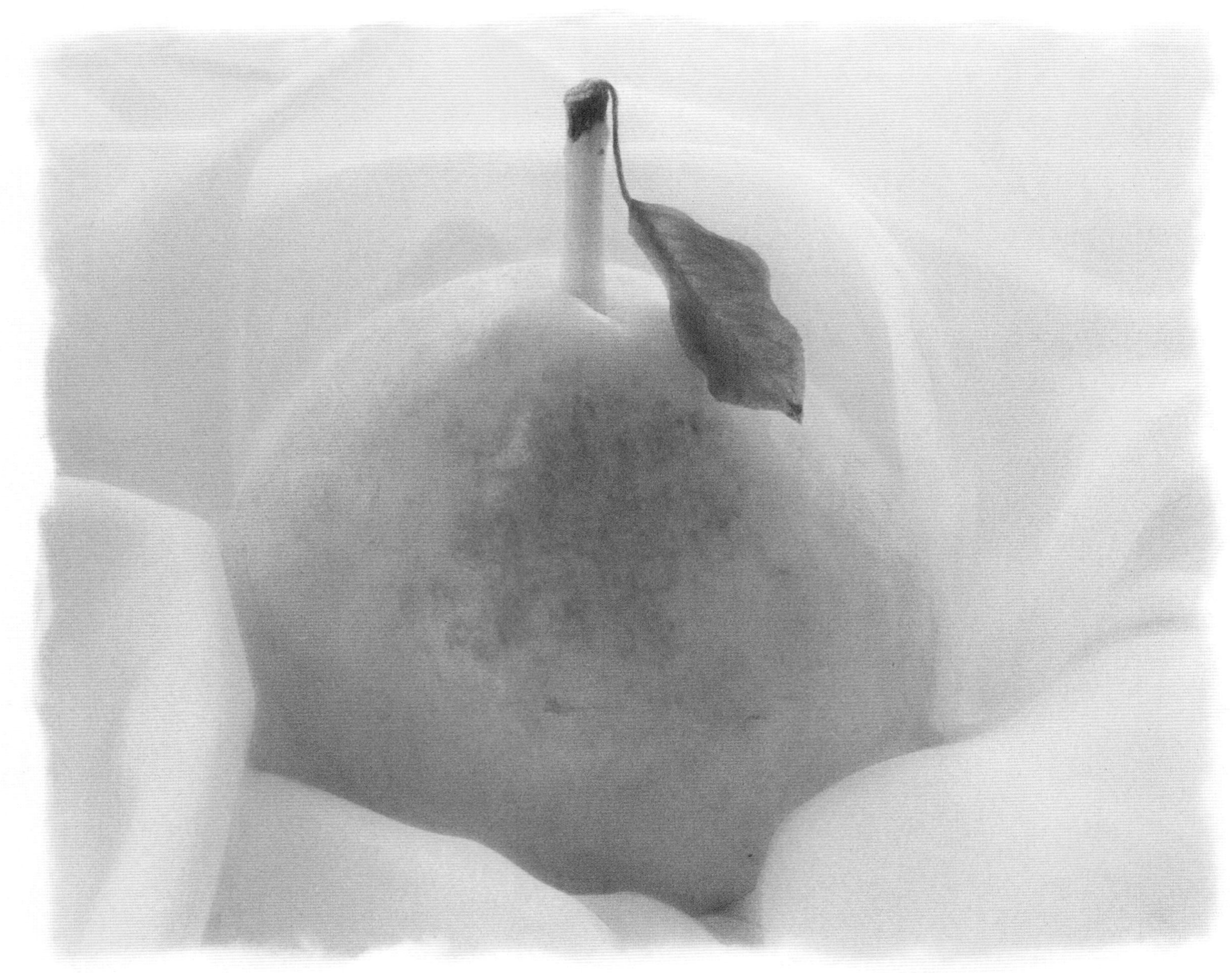

Pear

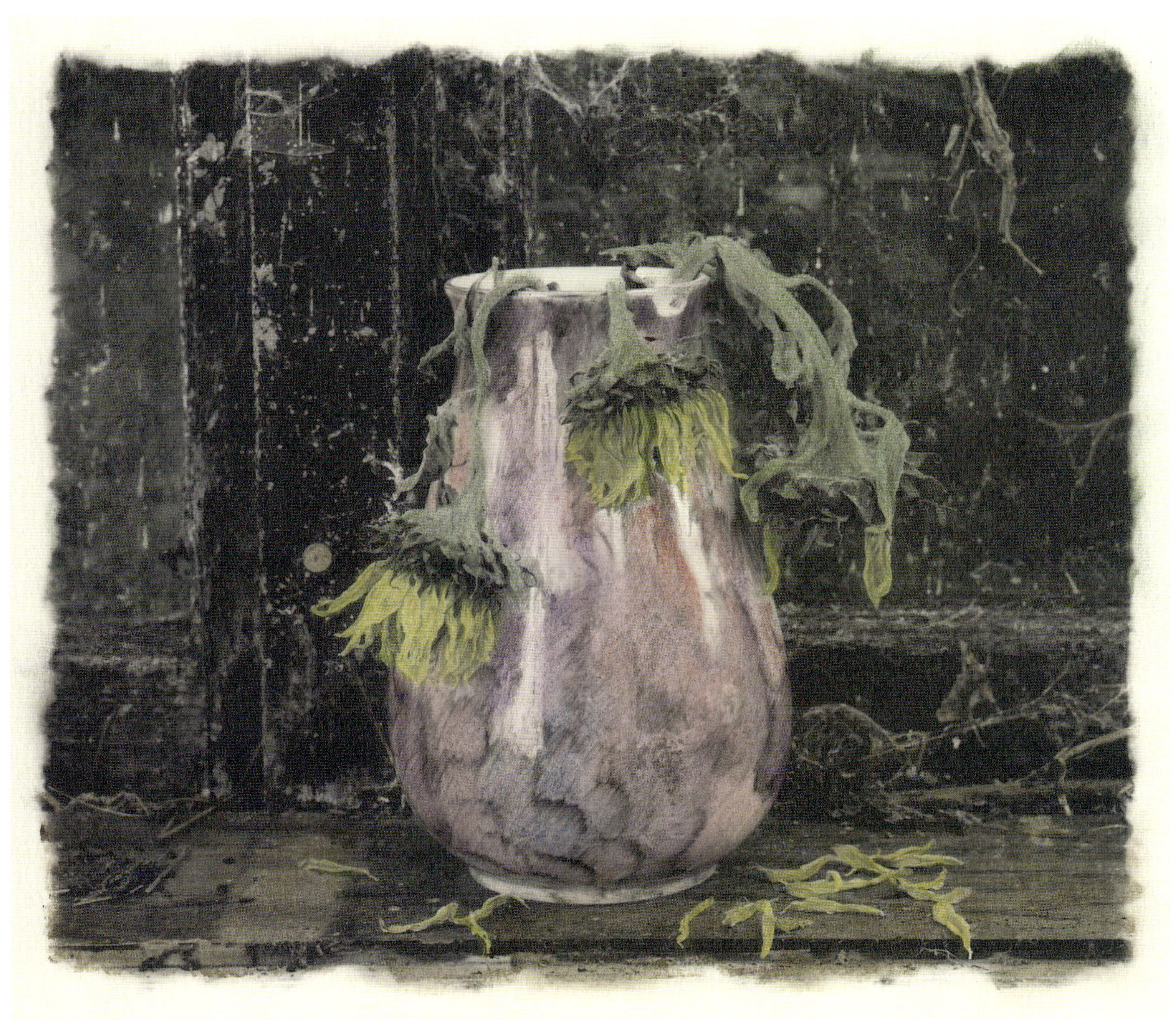

Better days past

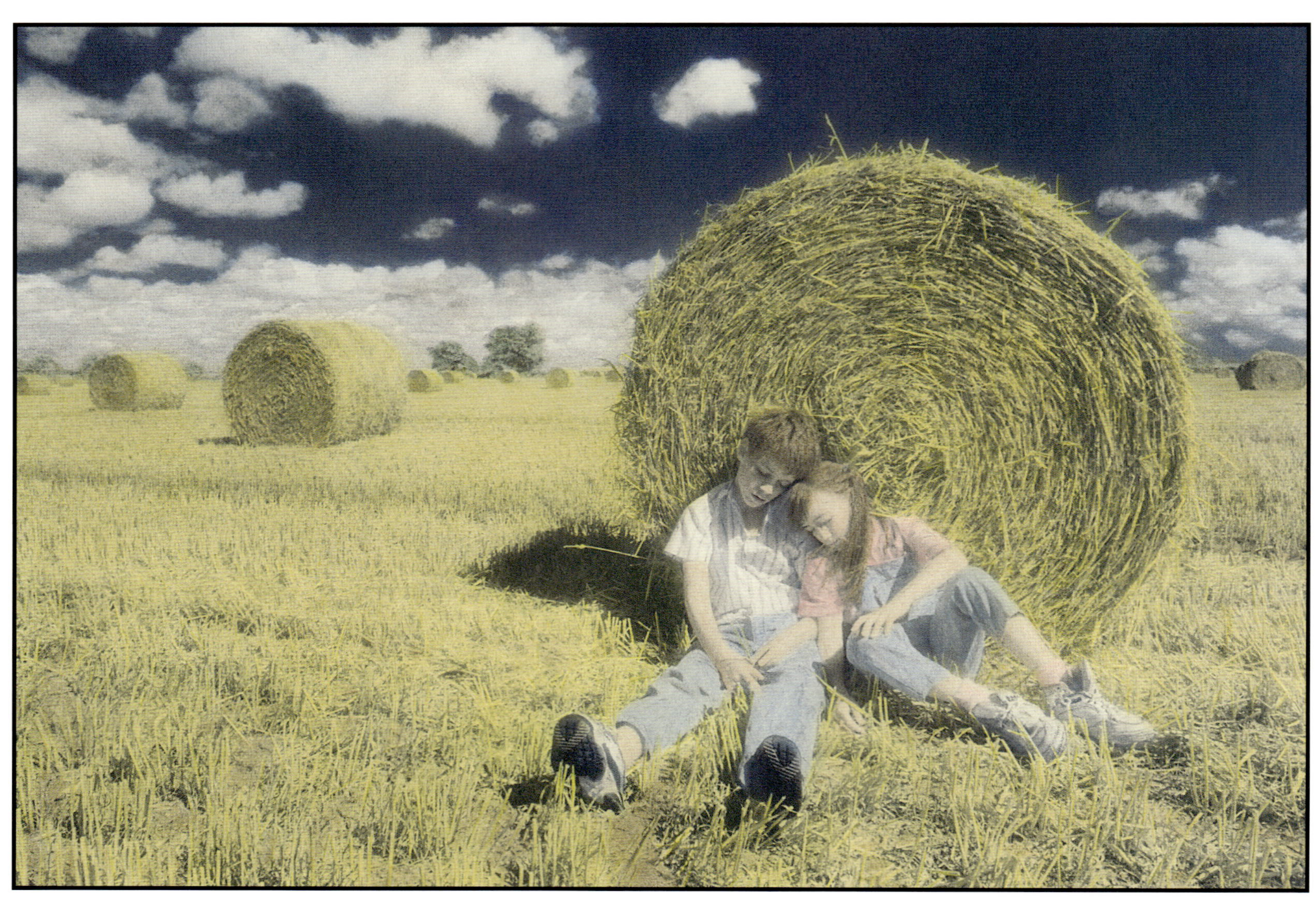

(above)
After the harvest

(right)
Jenny

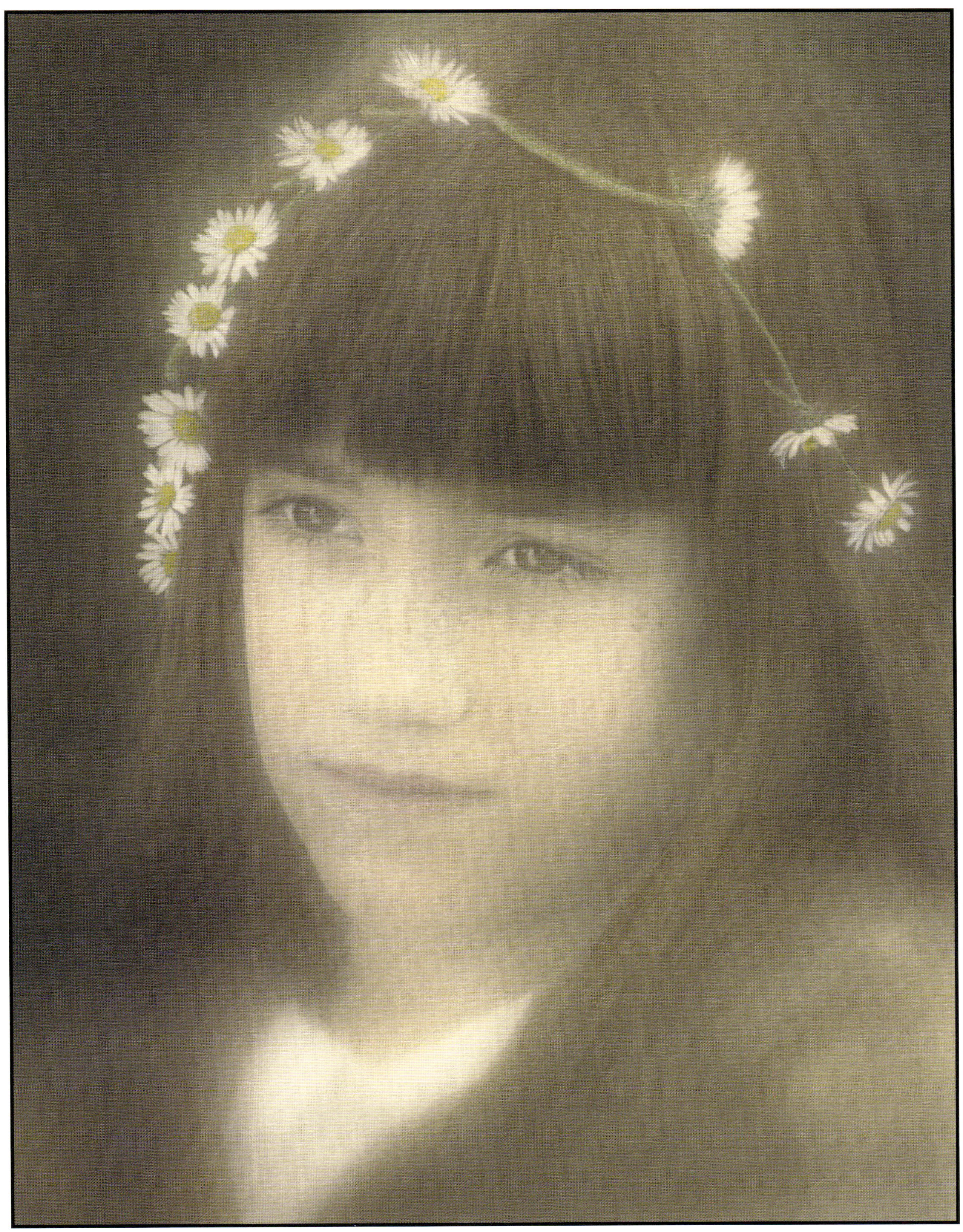

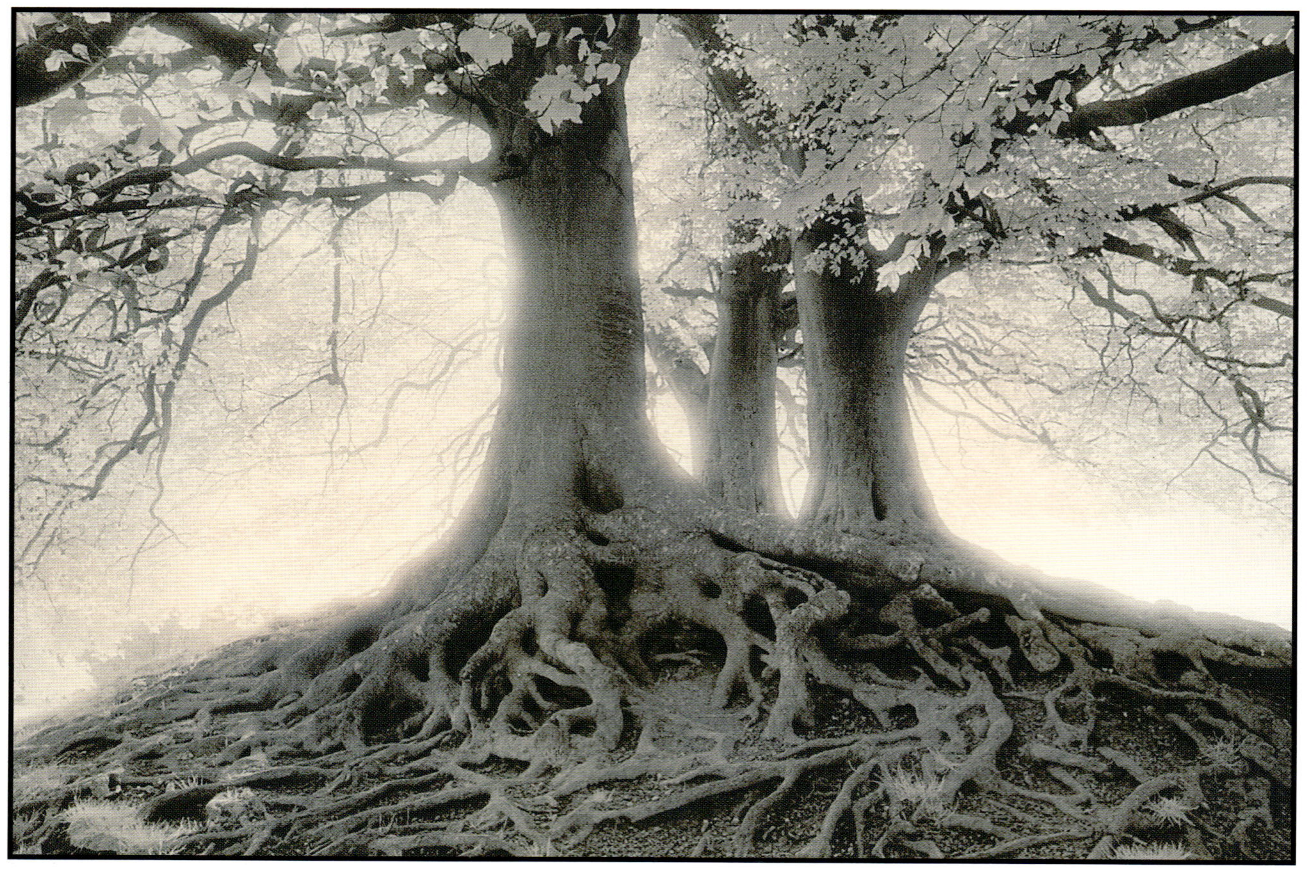

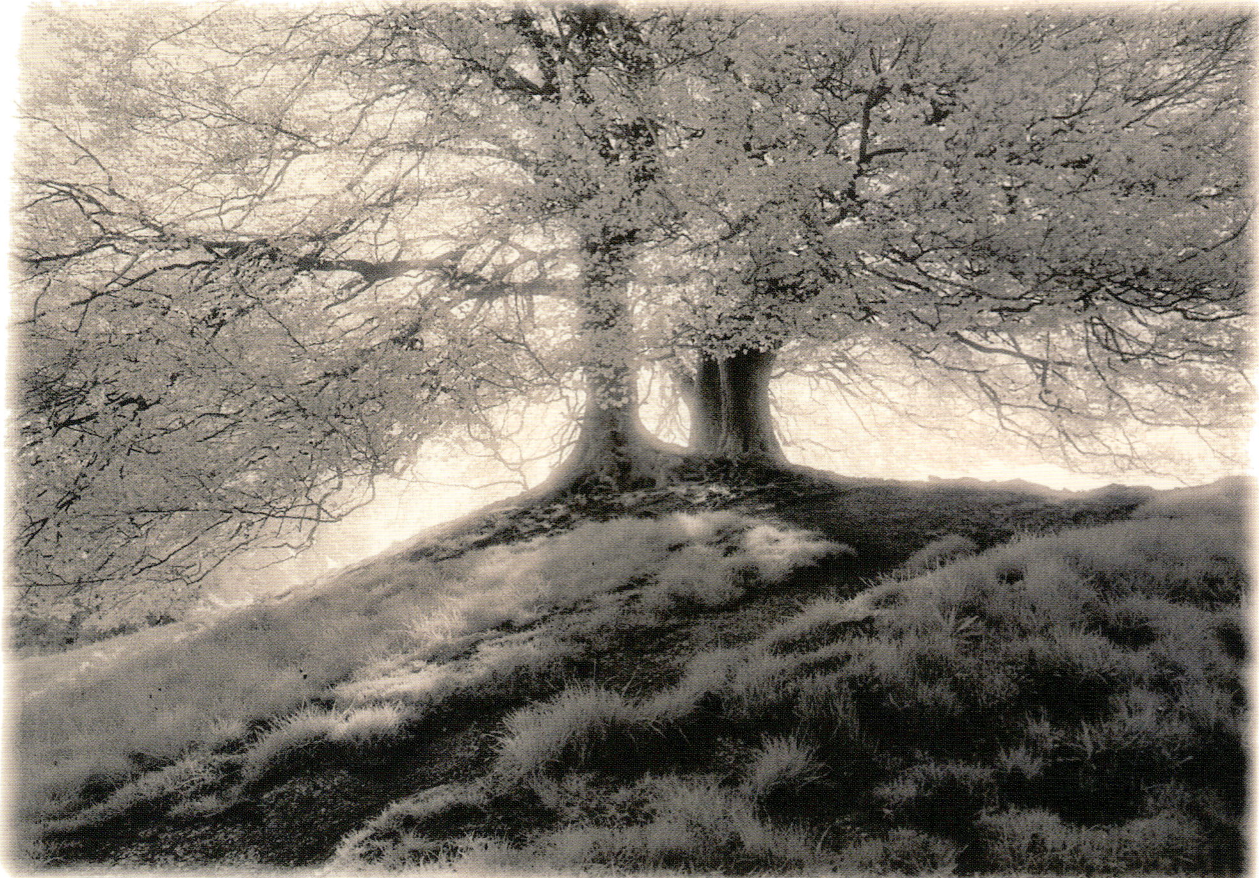

(top left)
Together

(top right)
The dream

(bottom left)
Trees on the hill

(bottom right)
Furzey

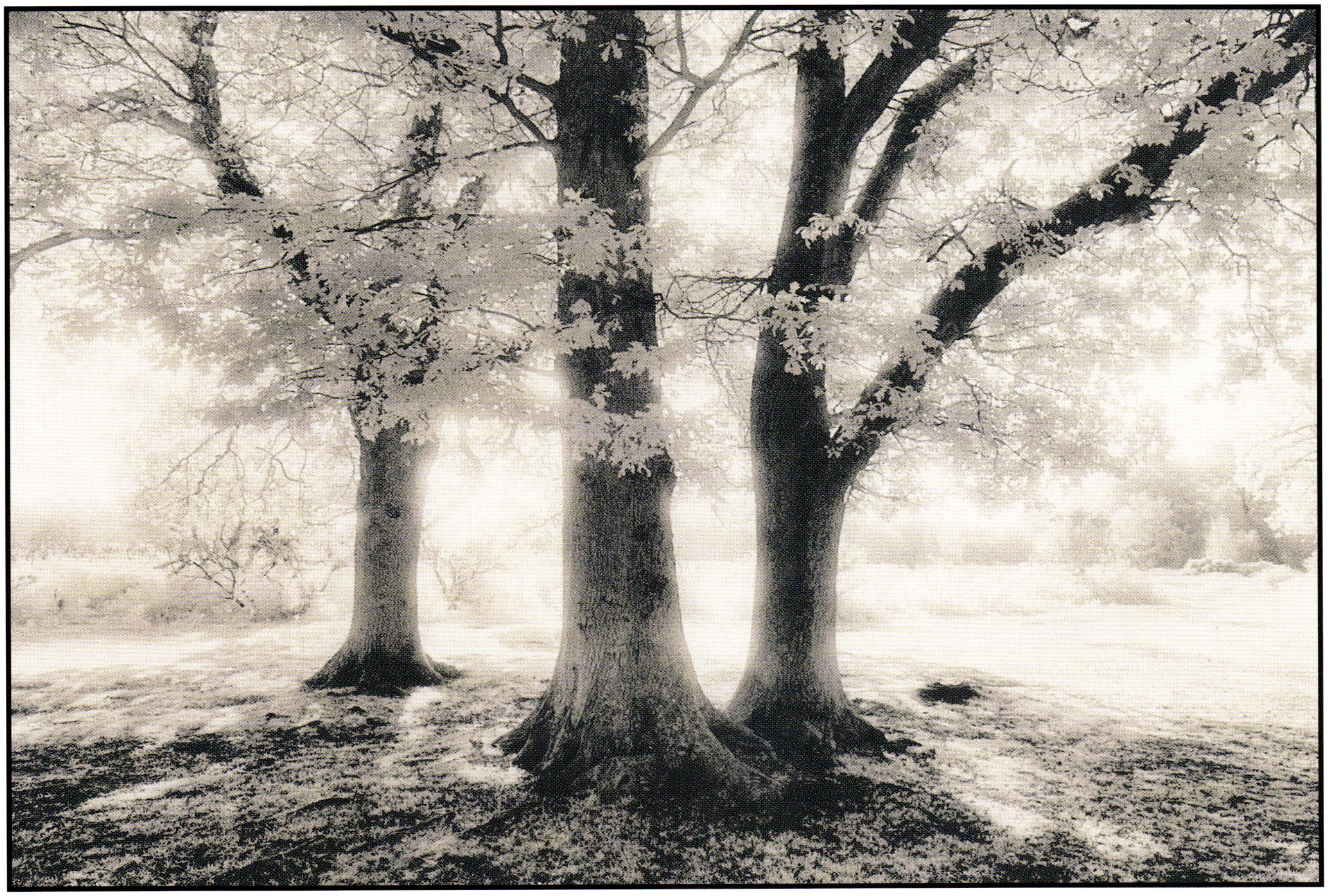

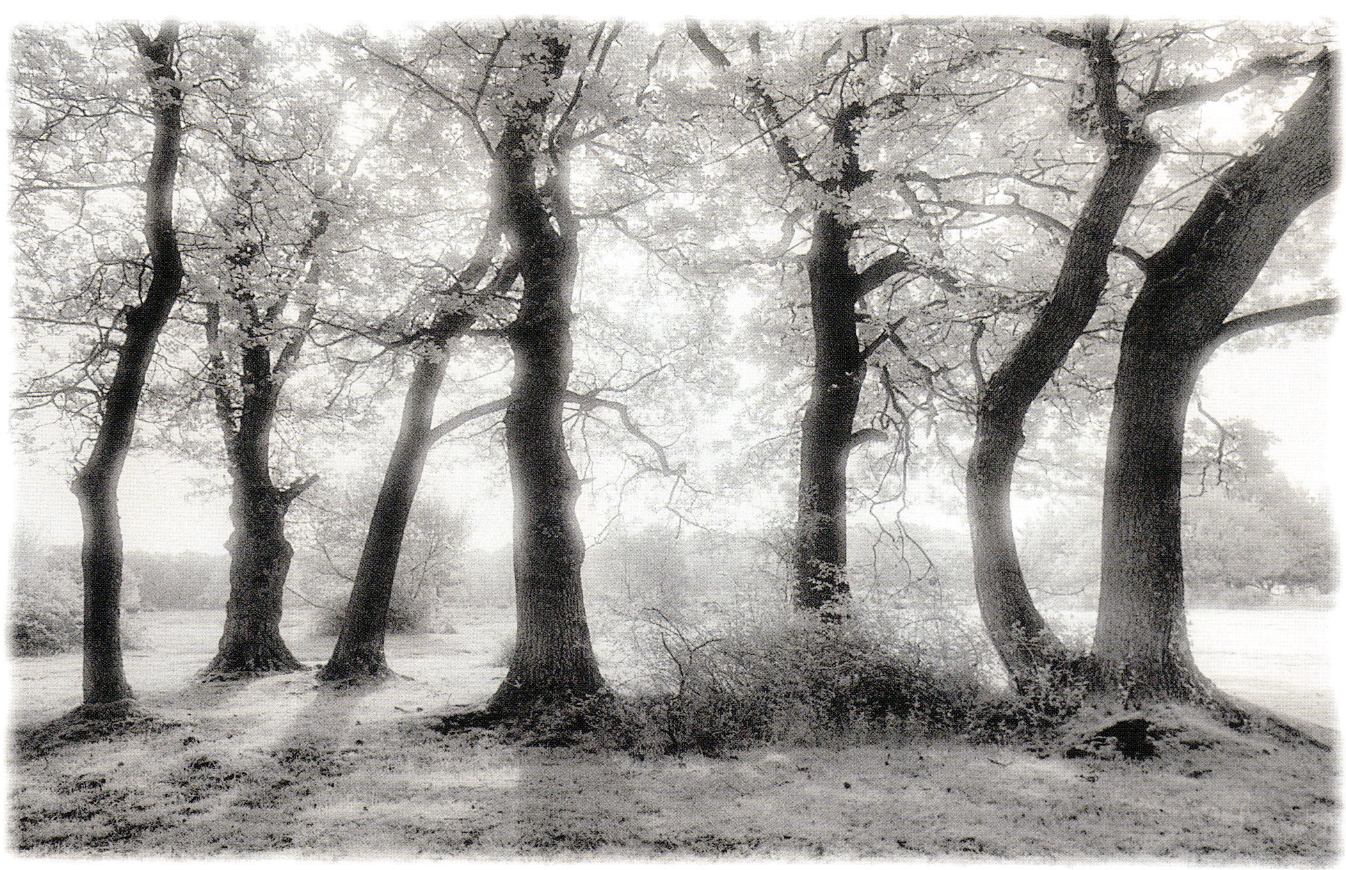

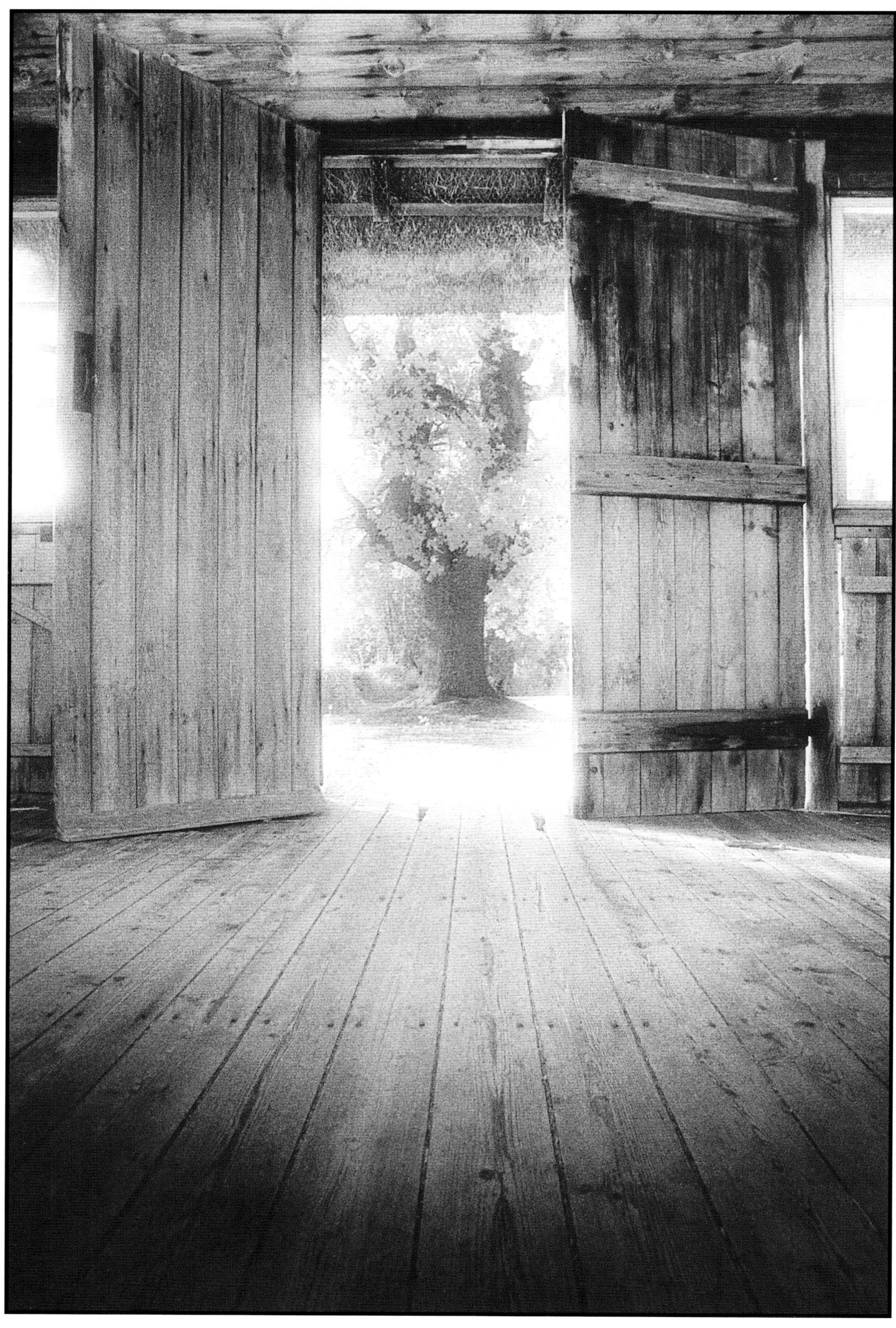

(left)
Invitation

(top right)
Autumn leaves

(bottom right)
All that's left

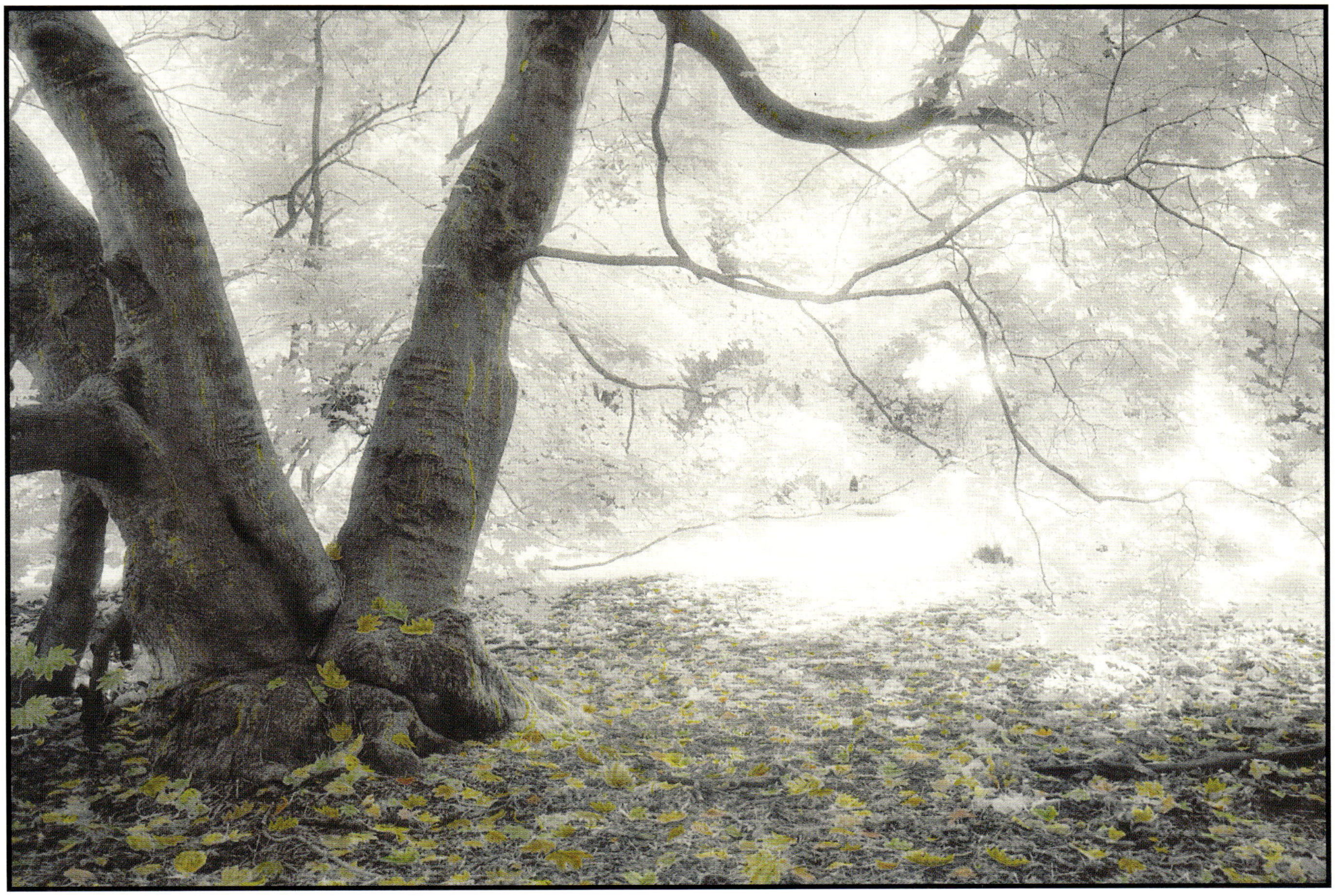

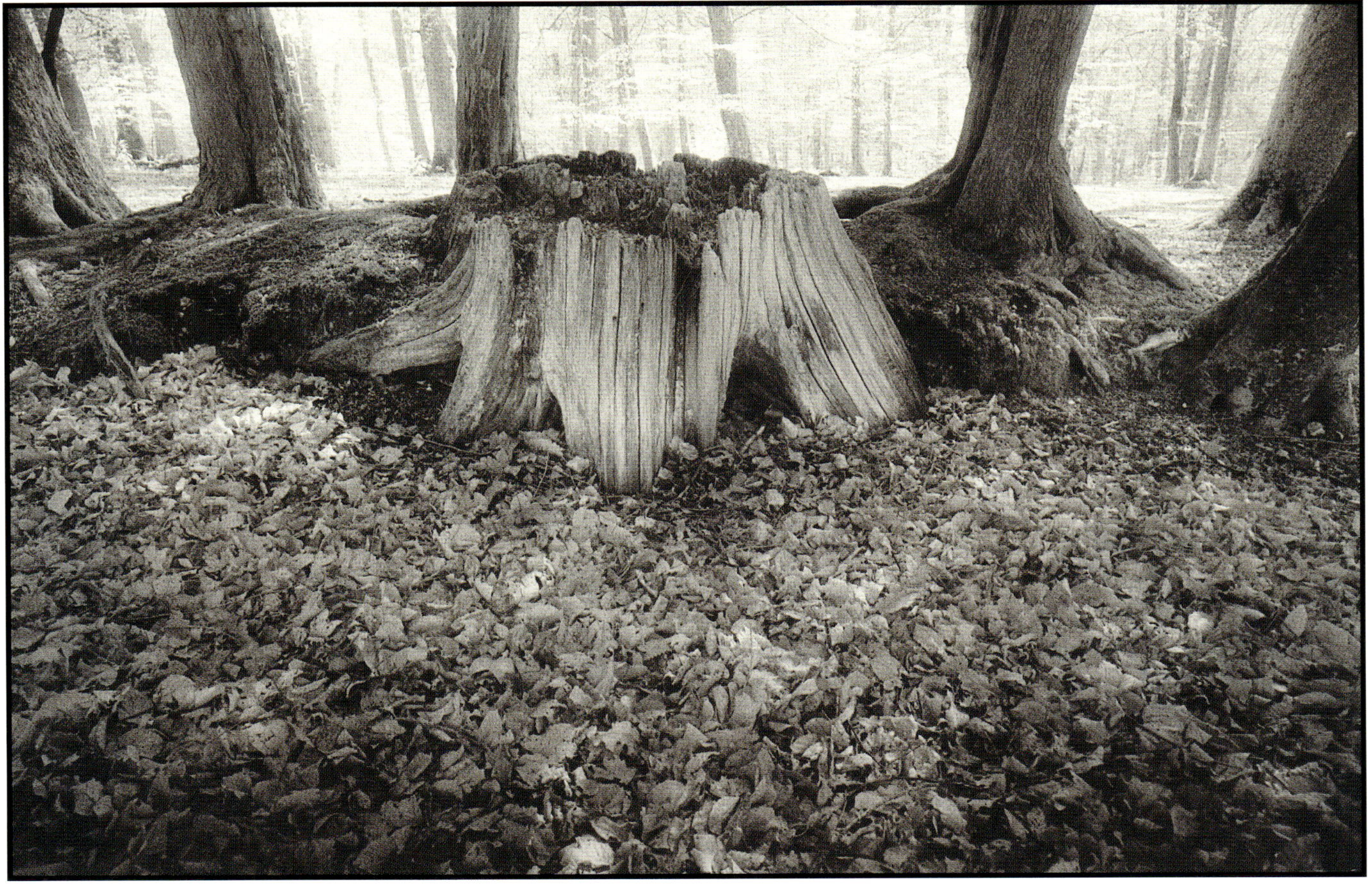

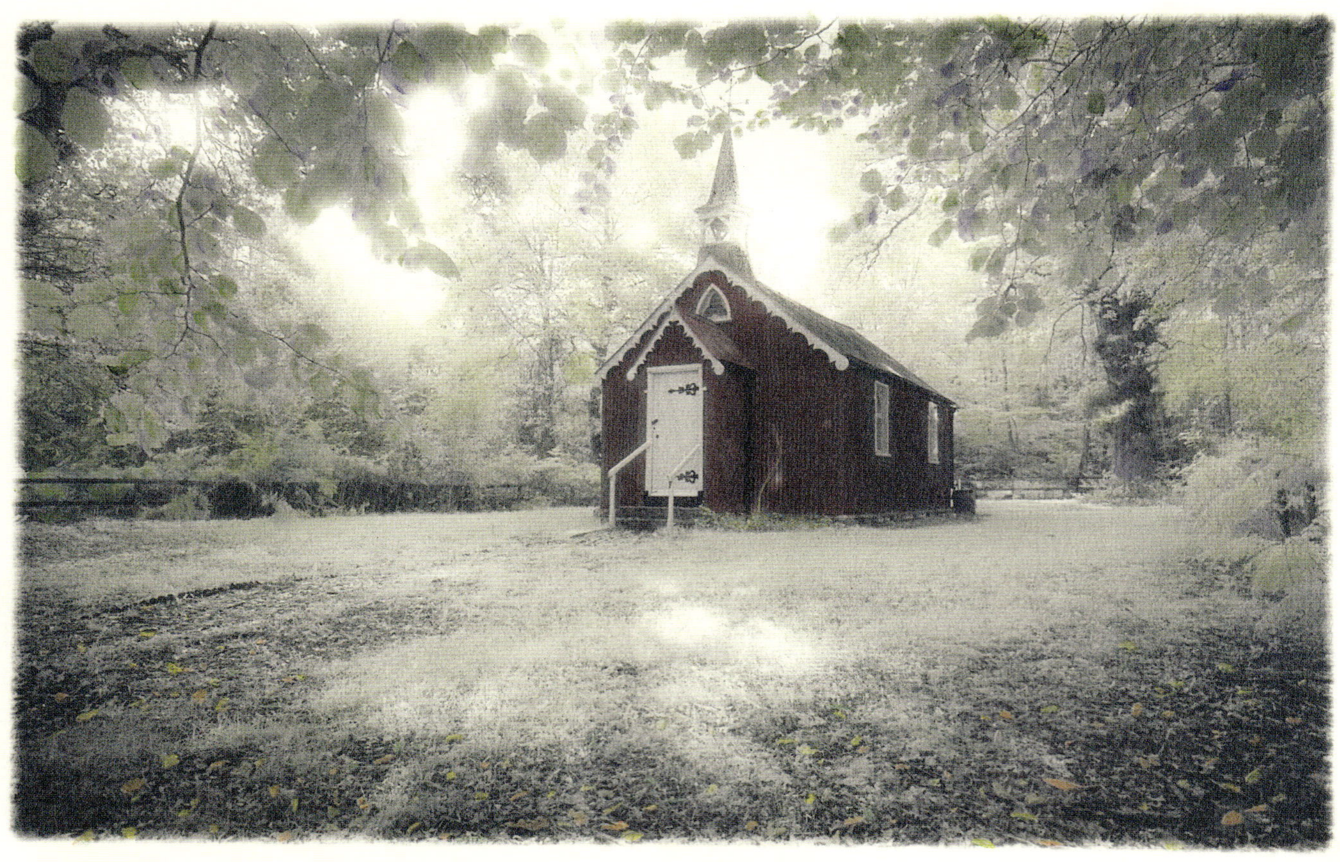

Romany Church

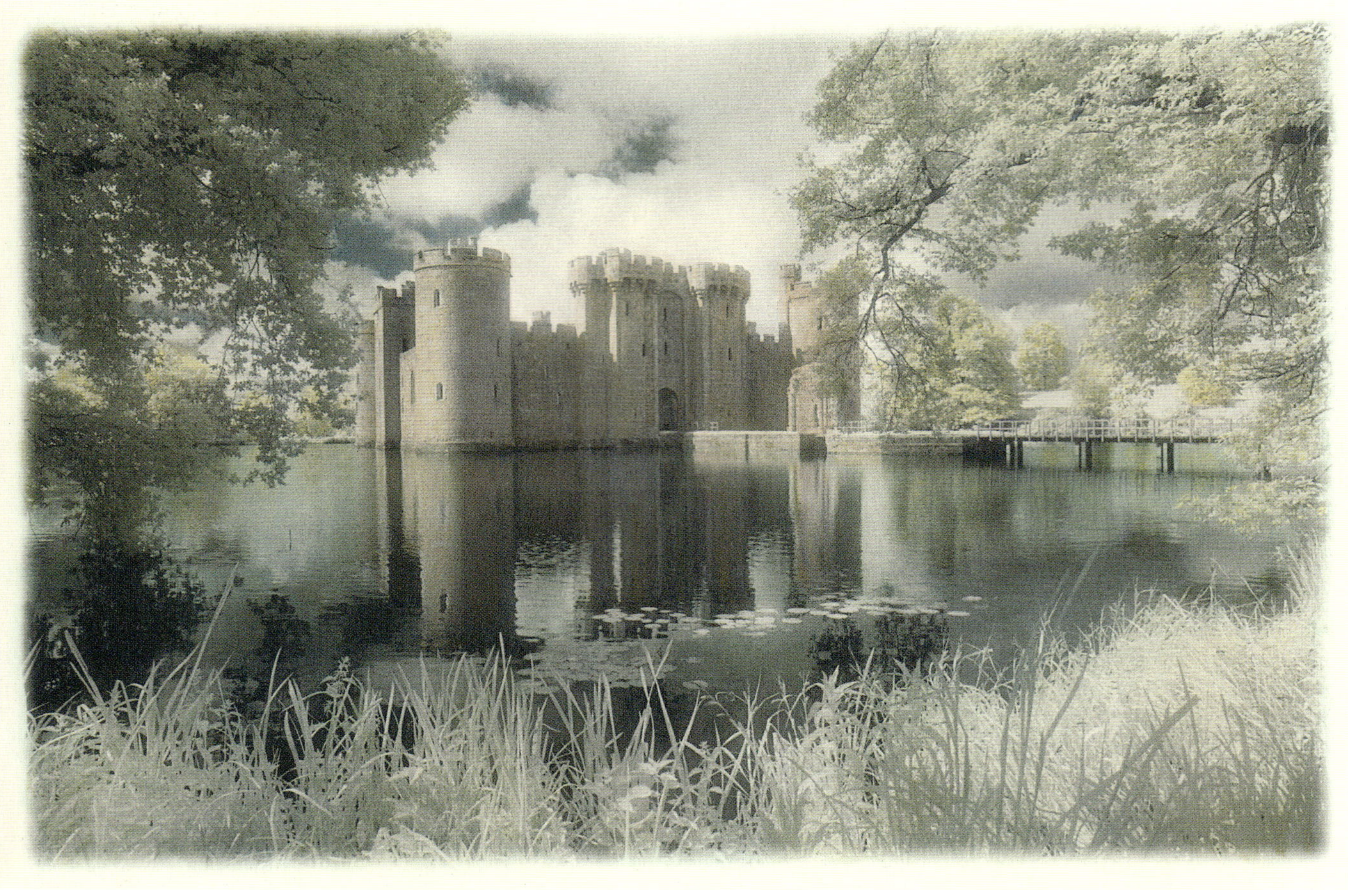

Bodiam Castle II

LITH PRINTING INTRODUCTION

Lith printing is an intriguing process that requires a different approach to printing. Usual darkroom practice is ignored, precise timings go out of the window, and patience is definitely a virtue. The resulting prints exhibit soft and delicate glowing highlights and gentle colourful mid-tones, contrasted against striking dark black tones. The effects can be subtle, or hard, depending on how the print is made, and stunning results can be achieved

The lith process involves over-exposing (by comparison with normal printing) your print under the enlarger, developing it in a very dilute lith developer and 'snatching' the print from the developer before complete development has taken place.

Lith developer is usually used to process lith negatives. In lith printing however, the developer is pushed to its limits, by massive dilution and then it works in a very special way. As you process prints, by-products of the development process add to the activity of the solution. This results in the dark tones accelerating rapidly – known as 'infectious development' – as the image forms, whilst the mid-tones and highlights lag behind.

In practice, the development process begins very slowly and at first the image appears and is quite difficult to see in the development tray. Gradually the darker tones begin to appear and then suddenly build-up faster and faster. At this point you need to be ready to snatch the print, aiming to capture strong dark tones. If the print is snatched too soon the shadow areas/dark tones have no punch, and if too late, they block up horribly with no discernible detail. This process can take anywhere between 6 and 30 minutes.

Ideally, if the balance between the development and exposure is correct, the snatch point you choose for the shadow areas is also correct for the partly developed mid-tones and highlights.

In this partially developed stage, the silver grains in the emulsion are very small and finely divided, and by stopping the development at this point you will get warm colourful mid-tones and highlights. These tones are particularly important in portraits and people studies where you may want to hold on to a flesh tone.

The developer produces the strongest lith results, and often the warmest tone, when slightly exhausted, particularly with the warm tone papers. For this reason, lith printers tend to save time by adding a little used lith developer ('old brown') from a previous lith printing session (say 50ml in each litre of developer). This will accelerate the maturing process. If you only have fresh developer, you can put a couple of sheets of heavily fogged old paper through the developer before starting your main lith printing session.

Variations in temperature of the developer can also affect the warmth given to the image, so an increase in temperature can be made if extra warmth is needed.

Never be concerned about the length of the development times, which will tend to increase during your darkroom session as the developer becomes progressively more exhausted. This appears more noticeable with some papers than others. When this happens, the developer either needs replenishment or replacement.

CHOICE OF NEGATIVE TO PRINT

When choosing a negative to print, think about what makes lith printing so exciting: the intense blacks working in harmony with delicate highlights. So chose a negative that will exploit these characteristics. Pictures rich in texture and pattern work well; portraits can be stunning, and, of course, infrared negatives are my particular favourite.

MATERIALS NEEDED

Not all photographic printing papers are suitable to use for lith printing, some of my favourites include:

Fotospeed Lith is a dedicated lith paper; a fibre based, double weight paper that has a lovely fine grain and a pale eggshell coloured base. It displays tones of peachy/yellow/brown and responds beautifully to toners, particularly selenium and gold. It is susceptible to 'pepper fogging'.

Kentmere Kentona is a conventional chlorobromide fibre paper, also double weight, on a white base and produces pretty buff/sepia/brown tones. (The original version of the paper emulsion, which contained cadmium, yielded pink and magenta tones and the lith prints in the book were printed on this).

Ilford FB Warmtone is a double weight, warm tone, variable contrast fibre paper. (There is no need to use contrast filters with lith printing as the contrast is achieved by exposure.) Lith processing gives cool browns and delicate ivory highlights. It responds well to selenium.

Other interesting papers are: Kentmere Art Classic and Forte Polywarmtone.

Lith developer. Lith developers are supplied as 'A' & 'B' concentrated solutions. Instructions provided with the chemicals show how to mix them for use with lith film, eg usually 1 part 'A' to 3 parts water, and 1 part 'B' to 3 parts water. For lith printing solutions need to be diluted more: to (say) three or four times the standard dilution. Solutions store well in their concentrated form, but once mixed, the working life of the developer is quite limited (maybe 2-3 hours). Lith developers which are very suited to lith printing are Fotospeed Lith LD20 and Champion Novolith.

Extra tips

- Because lith developing times are lengthy, the safelight must be good and correct for the paper you intend using. If in doubt, do check the literature supplied with the paper and/or run a safelight test;
- Lith prints are susceptible to marking and cross-contamination, so don't be tempted to prod prints or touch image area, and use corners only to pick up the print using tongs.
- Tray process your prints, rather than using a slot processor because you need to be able to see the changing development process and

LITH PRINTING INTRODUCTION

gauge the 'snatch' point.

- A small torch with a red filter over the front, used carefully, is useful to check the development progress.
- Fresh stop bath at normal strength is important to halt development quickly. (Not too strong as it can cause marks on the print).
- Fixing times need to be kept down to a minimum, both to avoid heavy penetration into the paper fibres and to avoid spoiling the delicacy of the highlights. Use fresh fixer normal strength.

STEPS TO MAKING A LITH PRINT

Pick a key area on your picture containing a representative range of tones, including shadows. As a starting point, make a test strip on your chosen paper using 'normal' print developer. From the test strip, pick out the best exposure time, using the mid-tones and highlights as a guide.

Next make a larger test strip, this time in the lith developer, remembering you need to highly overexpose the paper, eg try exposures of 2, 3 and 4 stops over the exposure determined by normal developer. Cut the strip in three pieces, so each piece has a selection of the exposures on it.

Develop the strips together in lith developer, agitating the tray continuously throughout development. Keep a close eye on the shadow areas where you want good blacks. Each section of the test strip will reach the critical point at a different time, by using three sections at once you can snatch each one at a different time, giving you a range of options to choose from.

Note: Assessing the snatch point can be very hard under normal darkroom safe-lighting conditions. It helps to use a small low power torch, with a red filter across the light, to peer at the print and check progress. However, to avoid fogging the paper, this should only be done near to the snatch point, not when the image first appears, and also not for extended periods of time.

At the snatch point put the strips straight into the stop bath; don't even worry about draining them off, just slide them quickly and smoothly into the stop bath. This will halt the development process and prevent further development. Remember to keep a note of the time you pulled each strip just to give you a guide for later.

After 30 seconds in the stop bath, drain off the strips and fix in the fixing bath. Switch to white light and study the strips. Look to see where you have a good balance between detail in the shadow and striking dark tones, in combination with nice mid-tone detail and overall colour warmth. This can be tricky as papers are affected by 'dry' down, where true density becomes apparent only after the paper dries. I give my test strips a quick wash and dry them in an microwave oven, which helps with this assessment.

Pick out the best exposure and, working from this, make a whole print. You will have a note of the time the test strip took to develop to its critical point and you can use this as a guide. But only a guide: the actual process time will vary slightly as the developer changes all the time. Use your visual assessment of the dark tones during development as your accurate snatch point.

Once you have made the print you can decide whether you need to make any alterations:

- If you find the print has built up the shadow areas very quickly and no highlight details have come through in that time, you have too much contrast. To solve this, you will need to increase your exposure time and reduce the developing time.
- If your print is too flat, lacking contrast and sparkle, you will need to increase contrast by reducing the exposure time and extending development time.

The rule with lith printing is to expose for the highlights and develop for the shadows!

Changes can be made to the mood and feel of the print by altering the exposure and development. For example, you may want a hard and gritty print, so by punching up the contrast and eliminating some of the midtones, this can be achieved.

If there are small uneven areas on your print where highlights are a bit too bright or shadowed areas just too dark, you can resolve this by localised dodging and burning-in, just as you would normally do in conventional printing. Burning-in tends to be needed less often in lith printing, usually taken care of by the heavy overexposure the print has already received.

TROUBLESHOOTING

Pepper Fogging

Fotospeed Lith paper is prone to 'pepper fogging', which looks like a scattering of black pepper over your print. This can be used to creative effect if that's what you are looking for! However, if this is not your intention, it can be very annoying. In order to eradicate this, you will need to introduce an additive into the developer. Sodium Sulphite should be added by making up a stock solution of 50gms in 500ml water. It is difficult to state exactly the quantity required because there are quite a few variables, but as a guide, add the same amount of working solution of Sodium Sulphite as Part A developer concentrate. Do not too add too much sodium sulphite or you will find your image is very flat, with little contrast and you are unable to get a good black. Add a little to start with, then check to see that the problem has been rectified before adding any more. As the developer becomes more exhausted, the pepper fogging may show up again, making a top-up of Sodium Sulphite necessary.

Potassium Bromide can also be added to assist with the removal of pepper fogging; this has the added advantage of altering the image colour. Potassium Bromide won't remove the pepper-fogging on its own and will need to be used in combination with the sodium sulphite. Mix up a stock solution of 50gms in 500 ml of water and experiment with the quantity, again basing it on the amount of Developer 'A' you are using. In this instance, try half of this amount and if this is not enough add a little more. (You can use a little less Sodium Sulphite if also using Potassium Bromide). Potassium Bromide will extend the development times. Fotospeed Lith LD 20 Developer contains a quantity of both Potassium Bromide and Sodium Sulphite powders for this purpose.

Border and Highlight Fogging

Extended development times can also produce border/highlight fogging on papers. This can be avoided by adding some of the additive detailed above (used to prevent pepper fogging) or by replenishing or replacing the developer, as the development times become longer.

Unwanted darker areas appearing on the print

It is important to ensure that you agitate the print constantly during development, otherwise the infectious development phenomenon causes unevenness.

TONING

Papers used for lith prints are often highly suitable for use with toning solutions and also can be handcoloured. Toning can add extra colour and increase separation of tones, as well as improving the archival permanence. The colour changes that take place with toners do vary according to the chemical make-up of the paper and the warmth achieved during the development: the warmer image tending to have a stronger result. Toning does not need to be taken to completion; the print can be removed from the toner once it takes on the colour you want. There are many toners available that can be used, two I particularly like using are selenium and gold.

Toned prints are susceptible to scum marks even after thorough washing, noticeable after drying. These marks can be removed by immersing the print in a 3% acetic acid solution for 30 seconds. They must then be thoroughly washed.

CONCLUSION

Remember there are so many variables that can affect the outcome of the prints and some experimentation is necessary to realise the potential of the technique. Make notes of what you do and where possible try to change just one variable at a time. Lots of time and patience is vital when lith printing, so I always have a comfy chair in the darkroom and music to listen to!

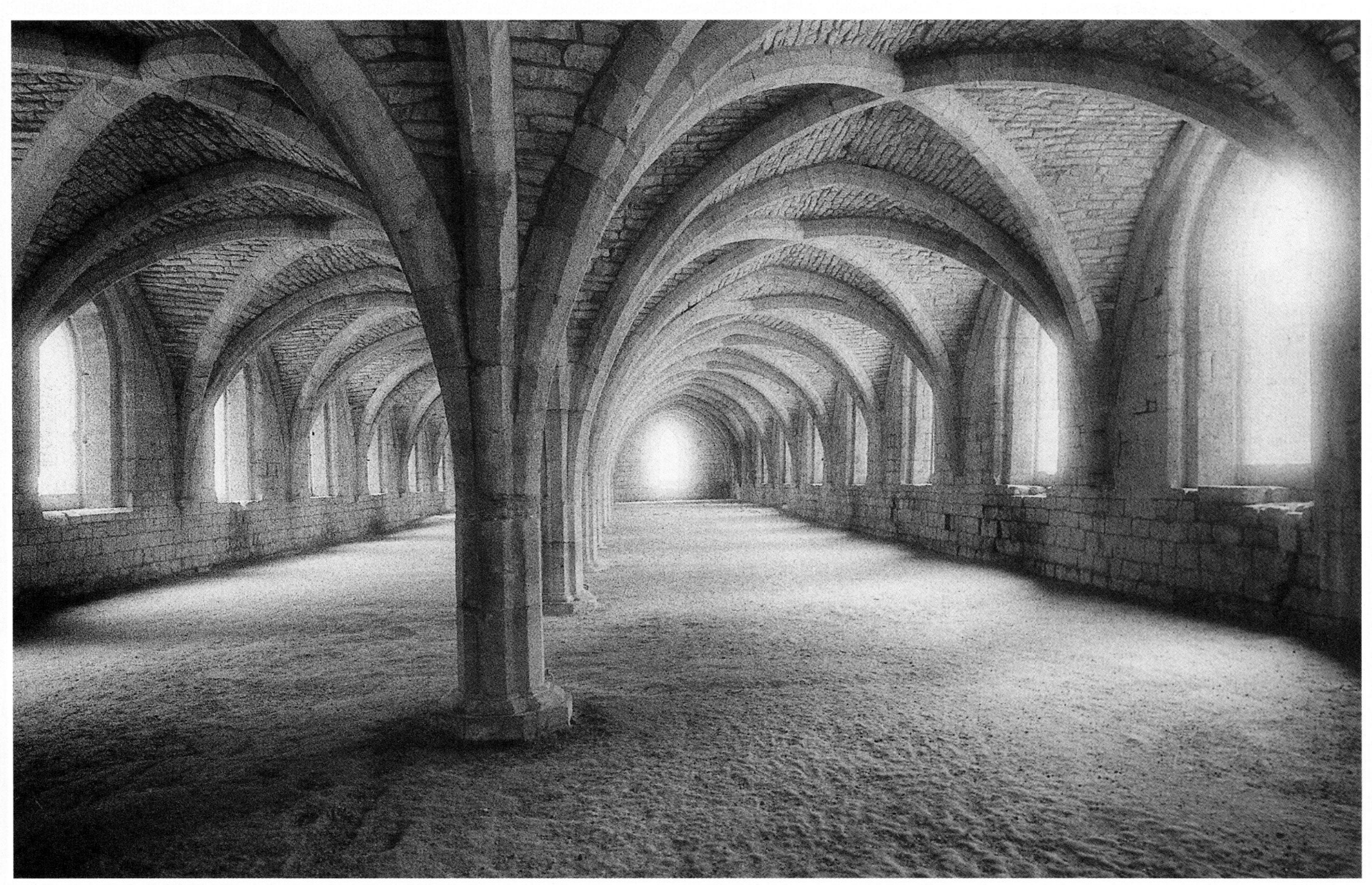

Fountains Abbey

MONOCHROME PORTFOLIO III

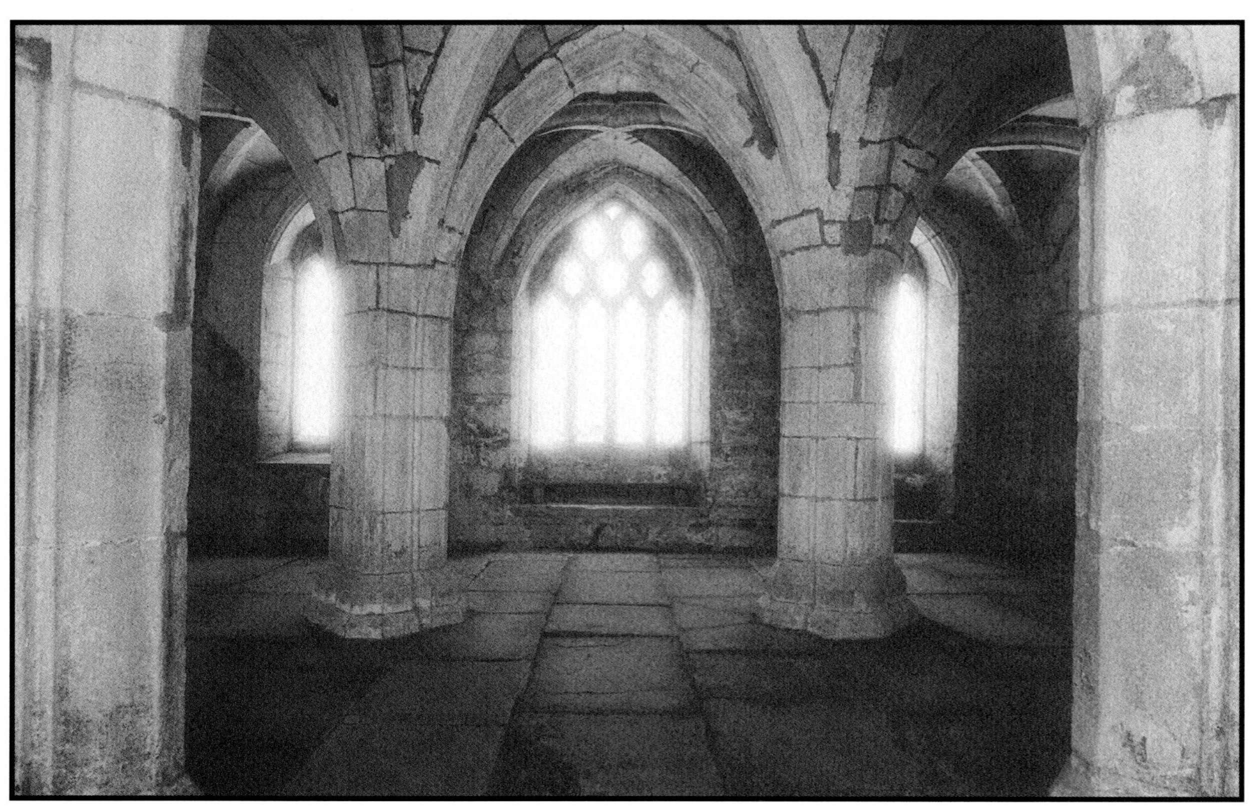

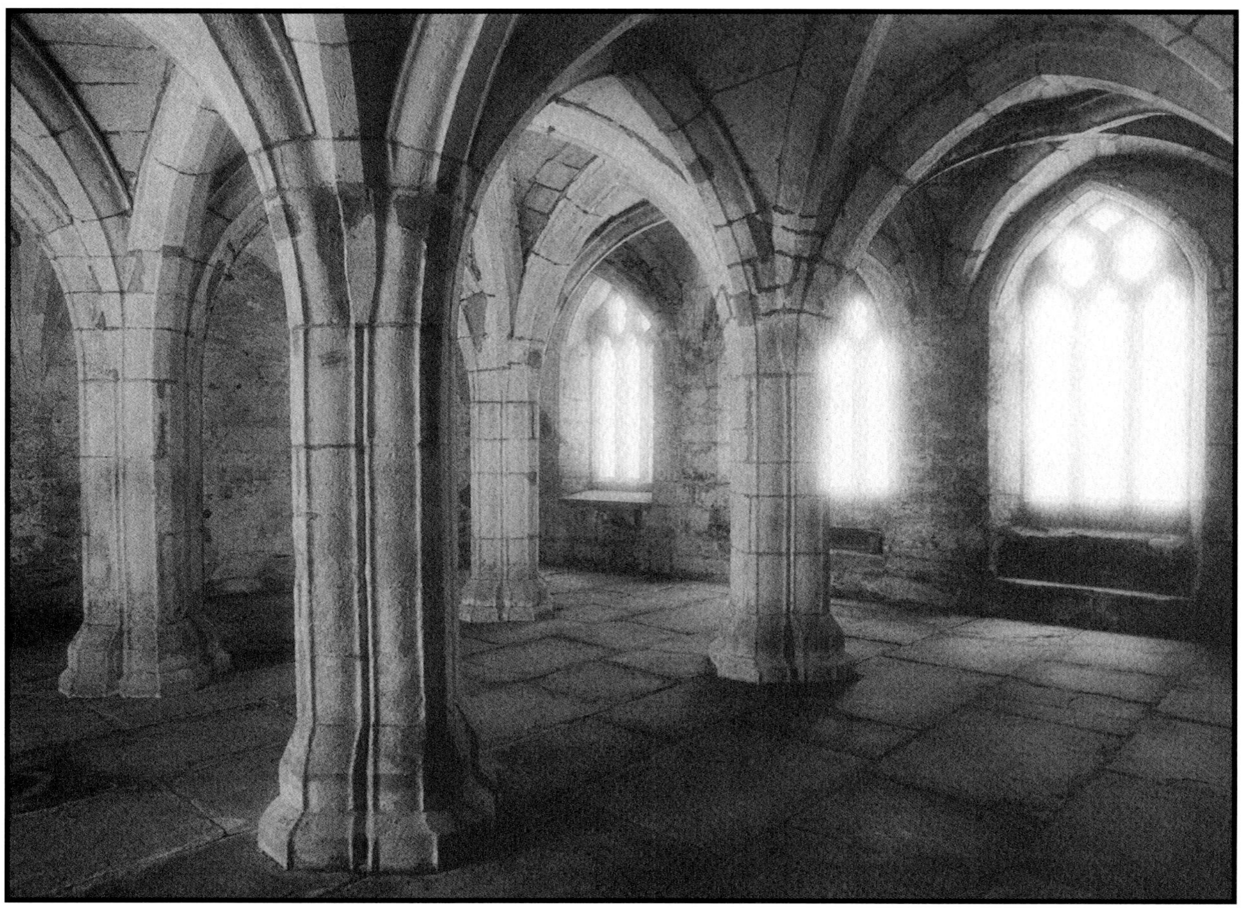

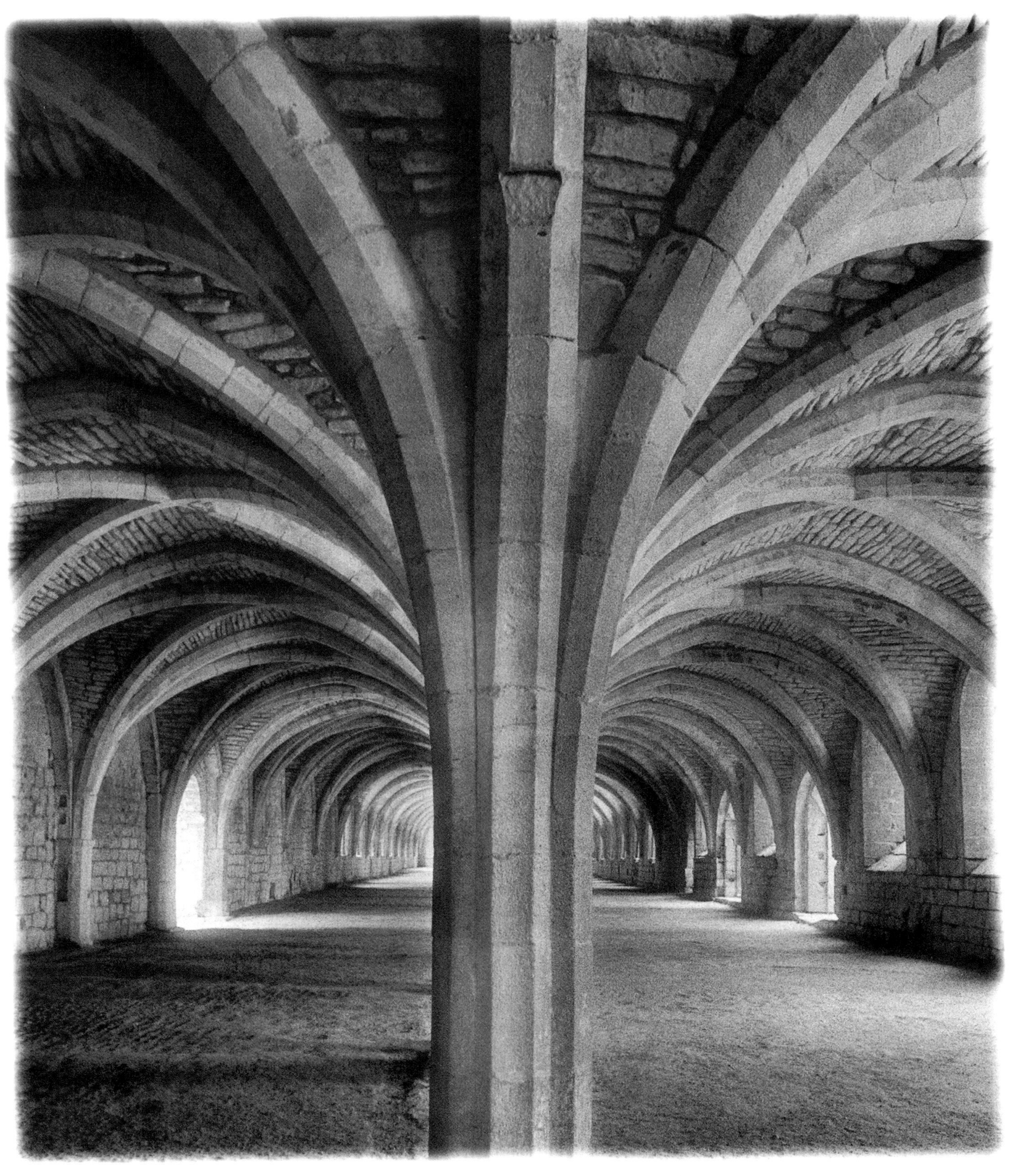

(above) **Symmetry**
(top left) **Abbey I** (bottom left) **Abbey II**

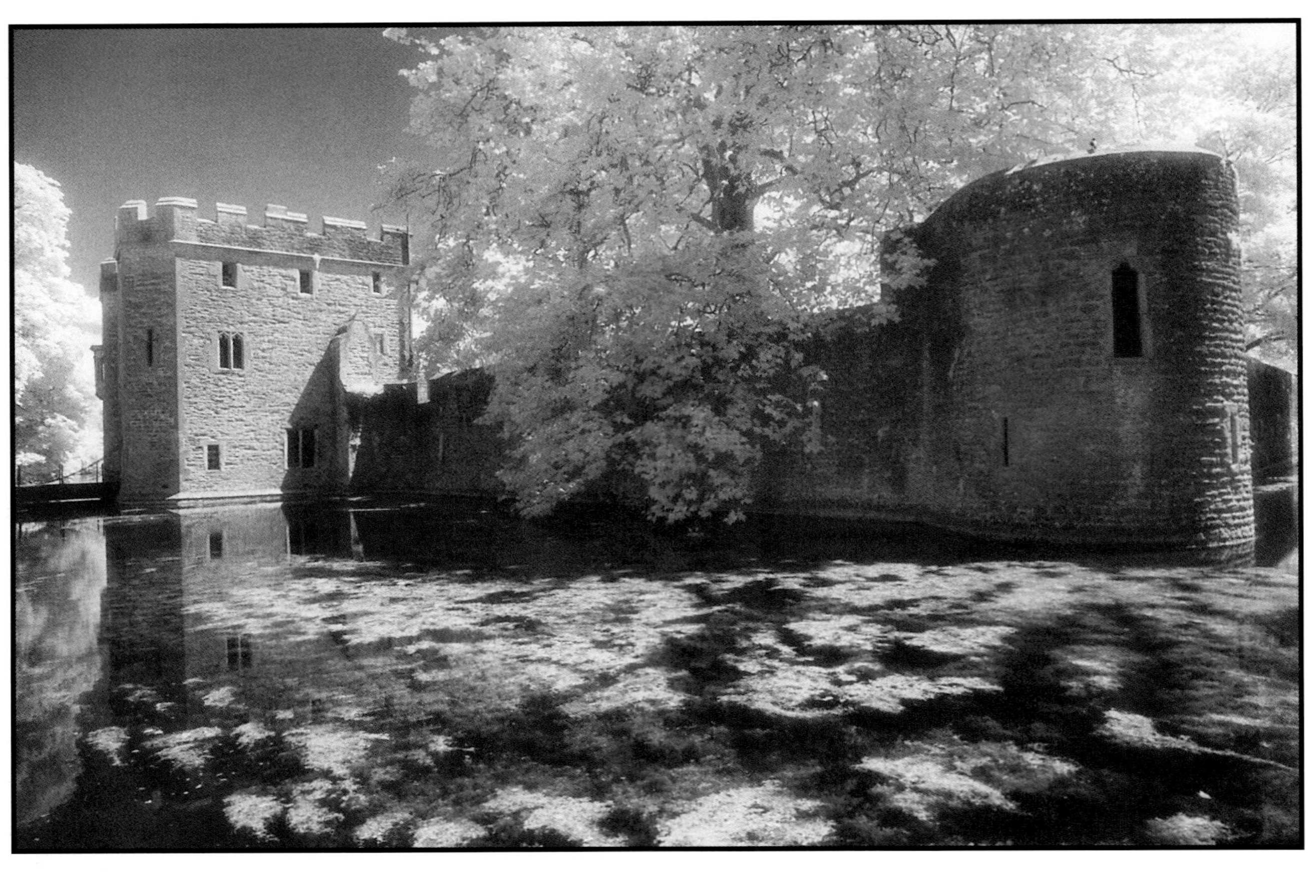

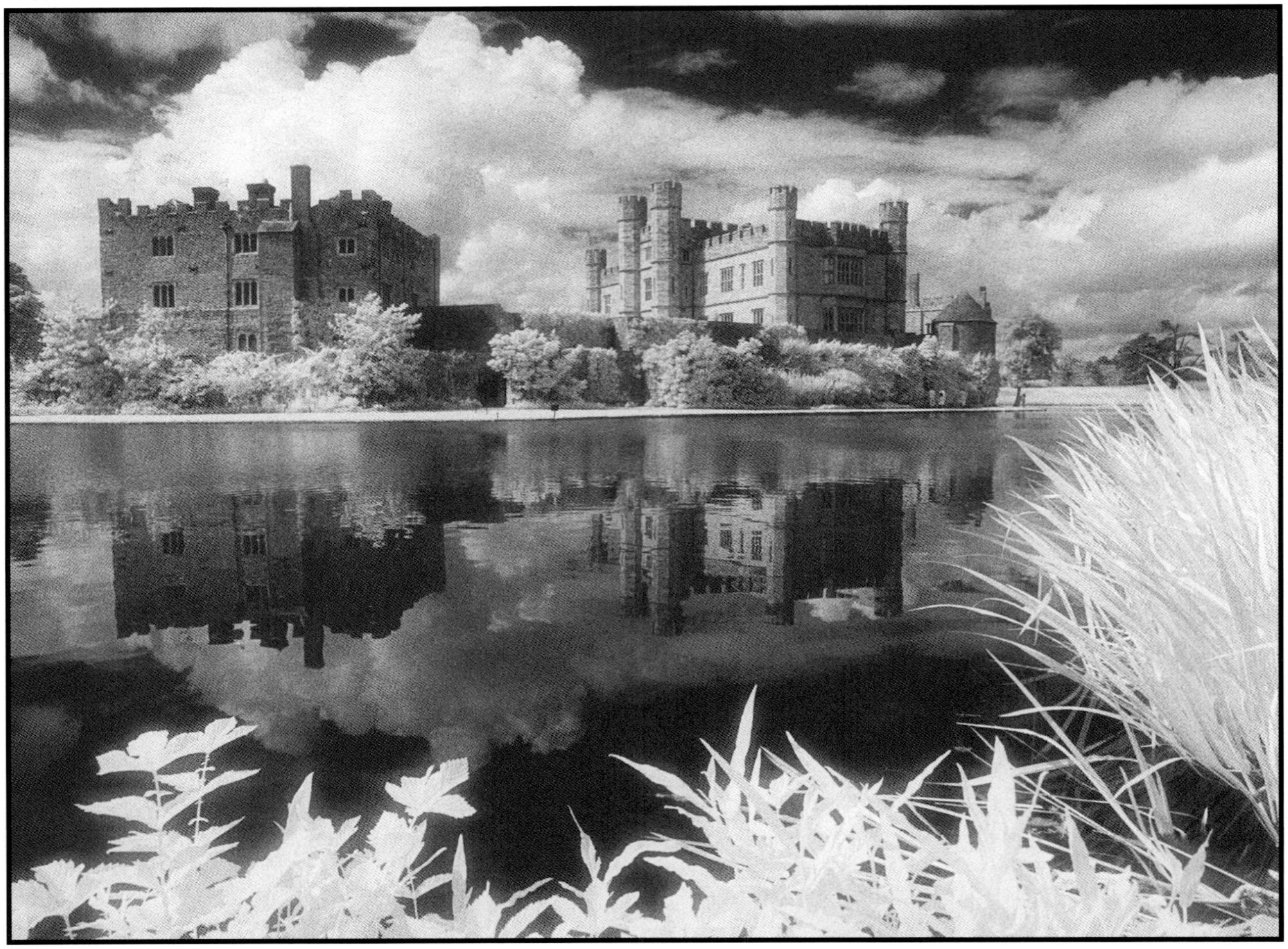

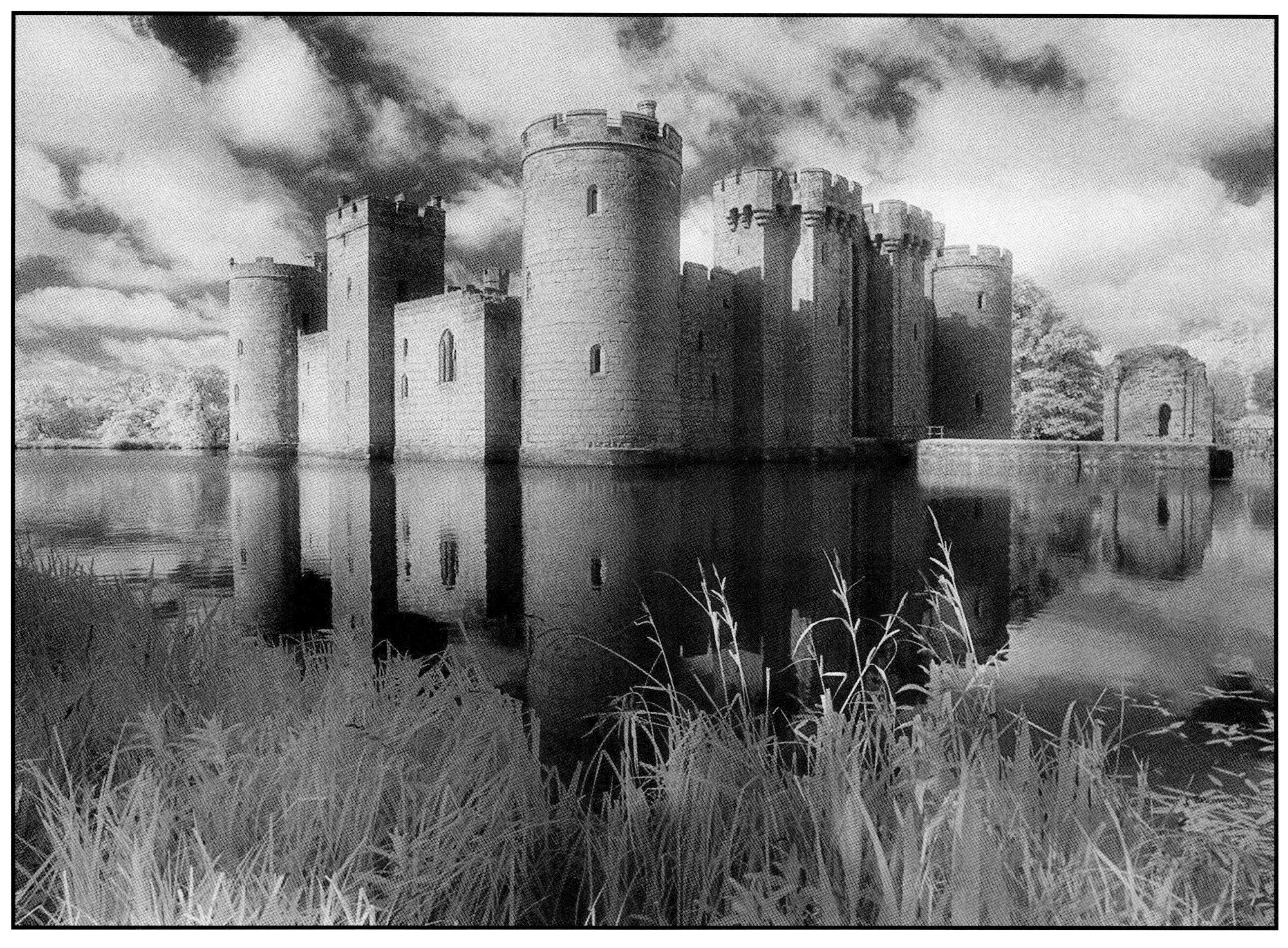

(above)
Bodiam Castle

(top left)
Bishops Place

(bottom left)
Leeds Castle

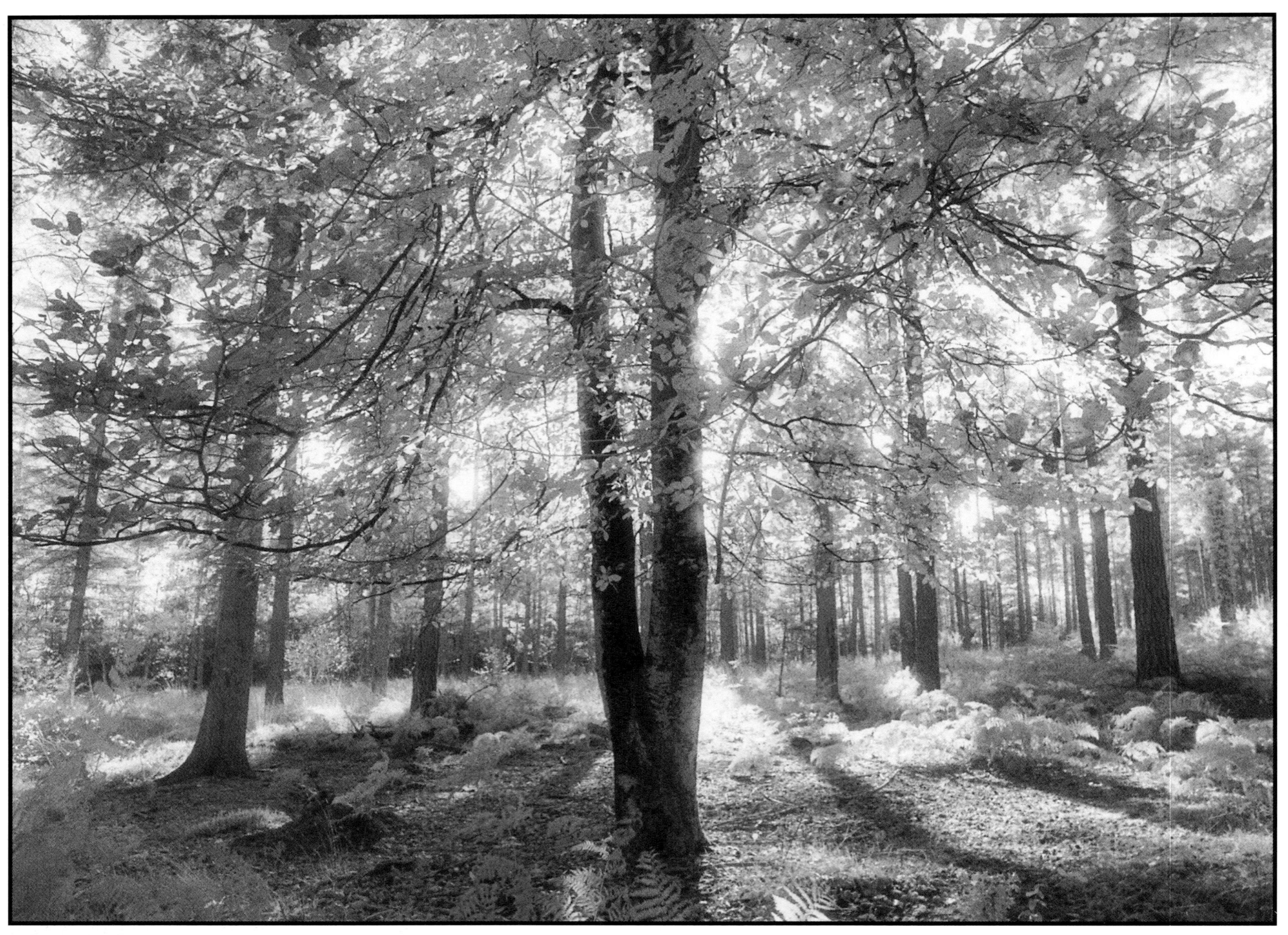

(above)
Moonhills

(top right)
Avebury

(bottom right)
Roots

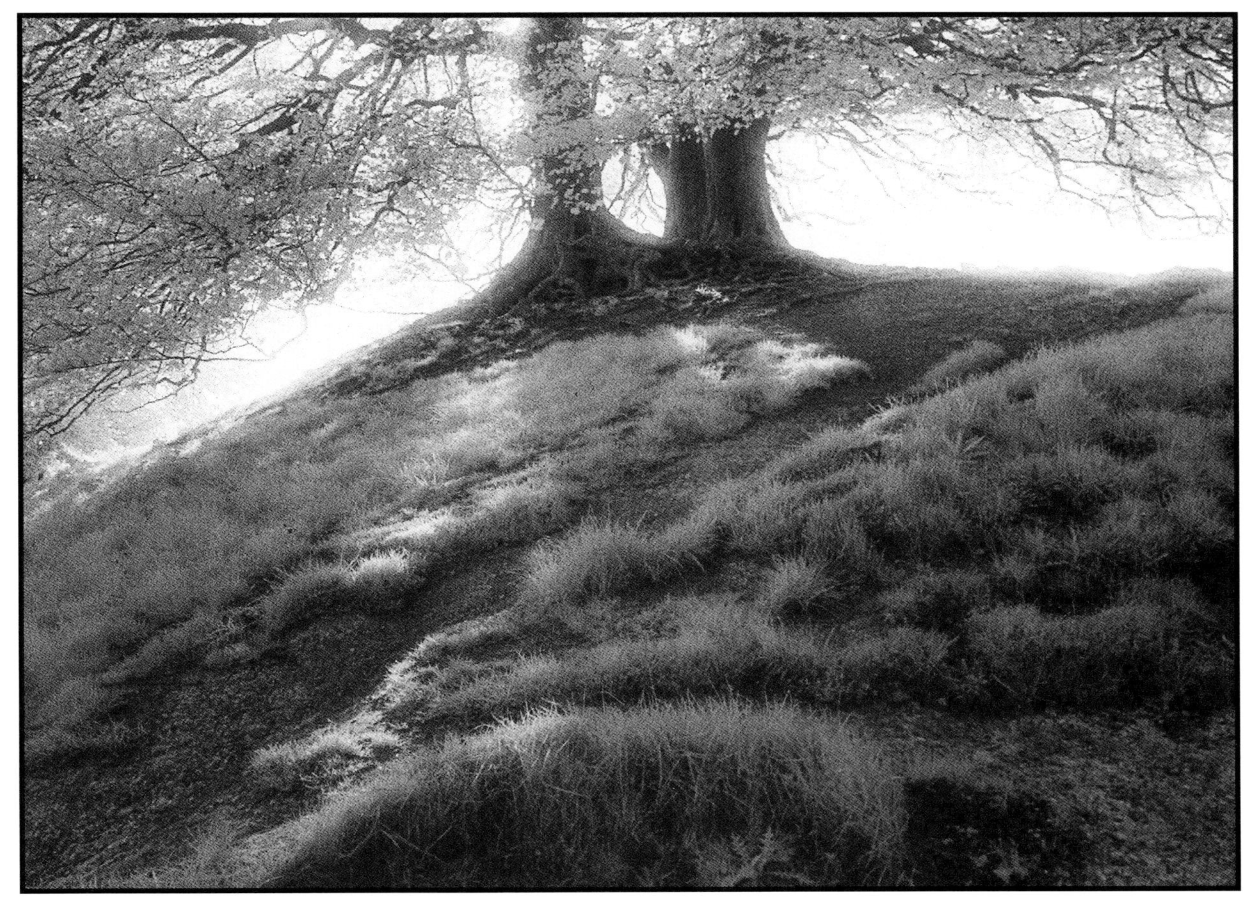

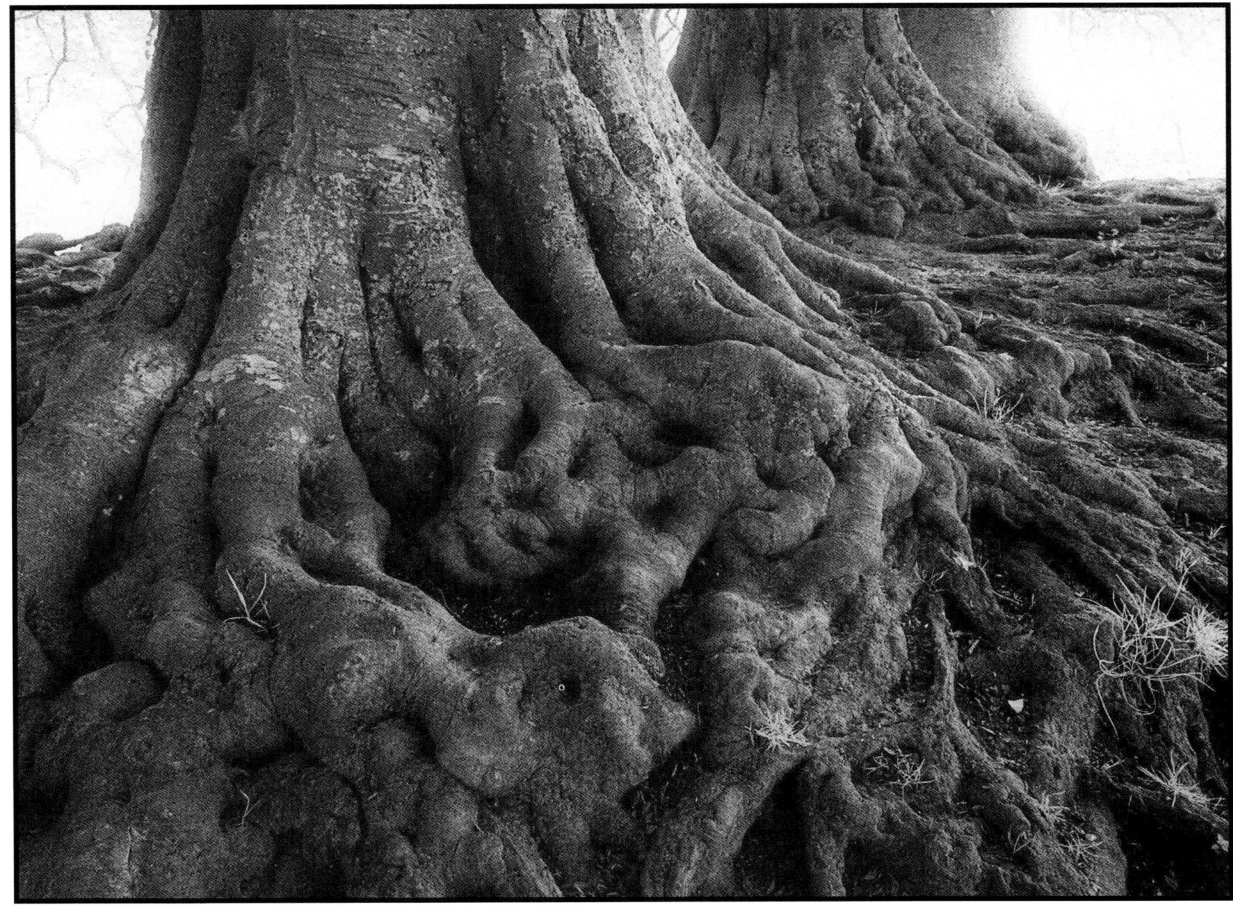

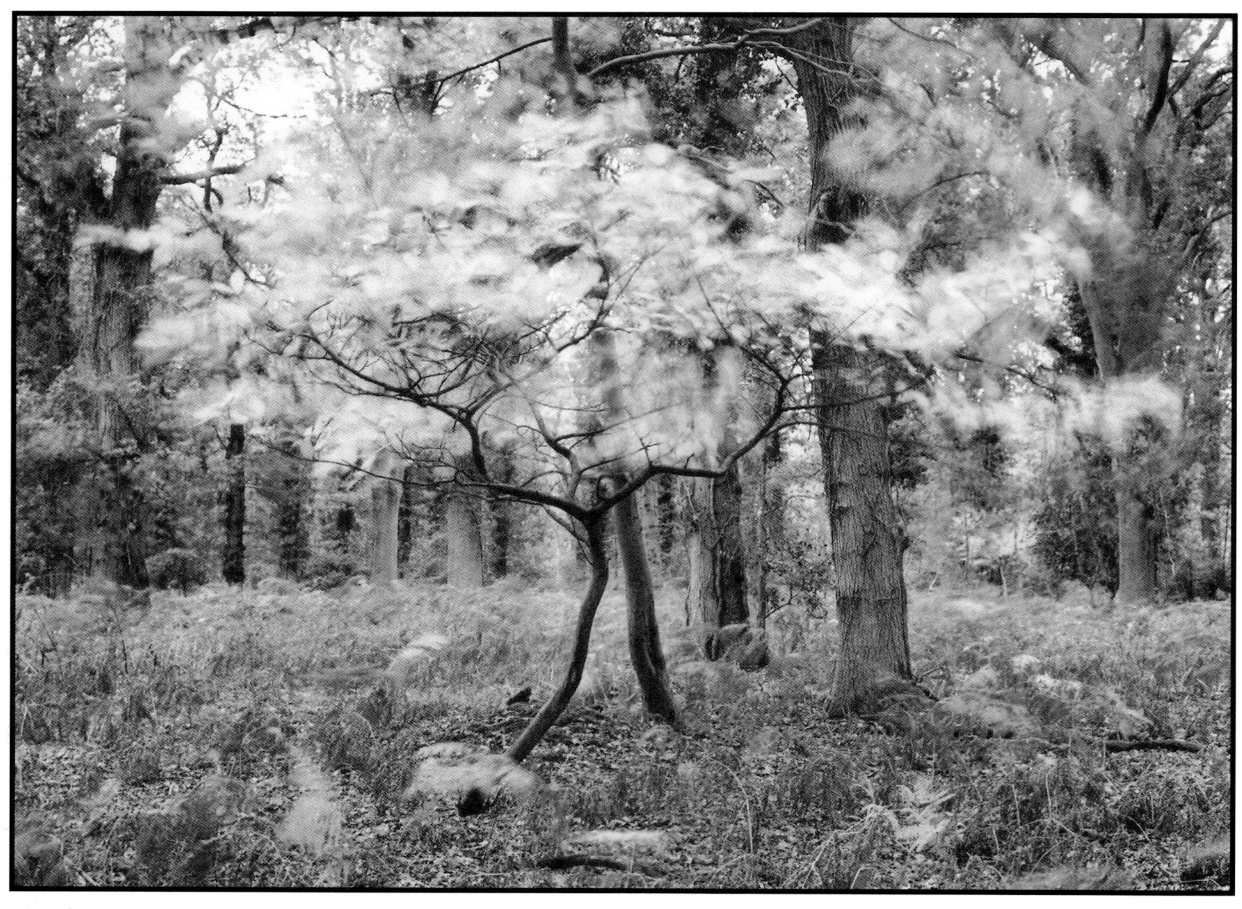

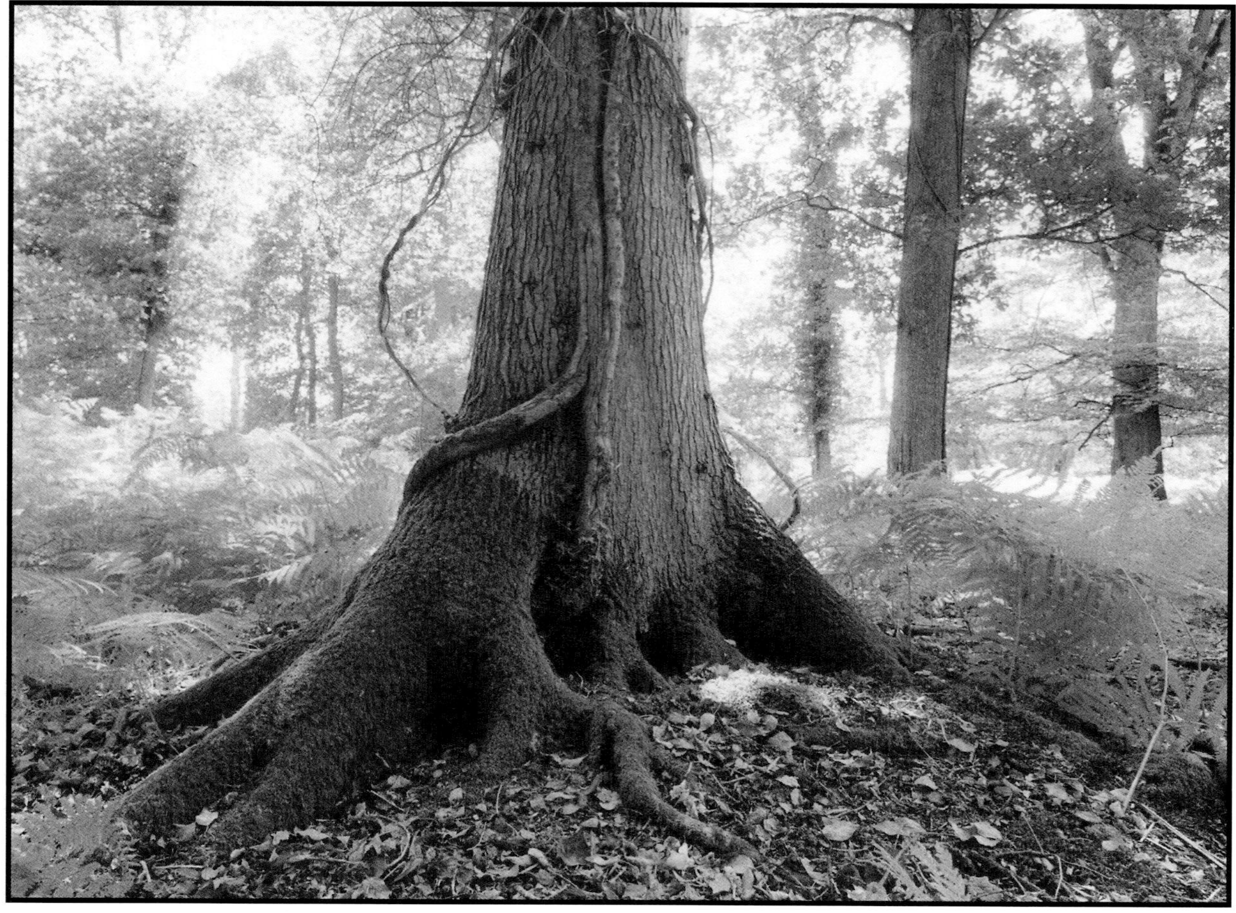

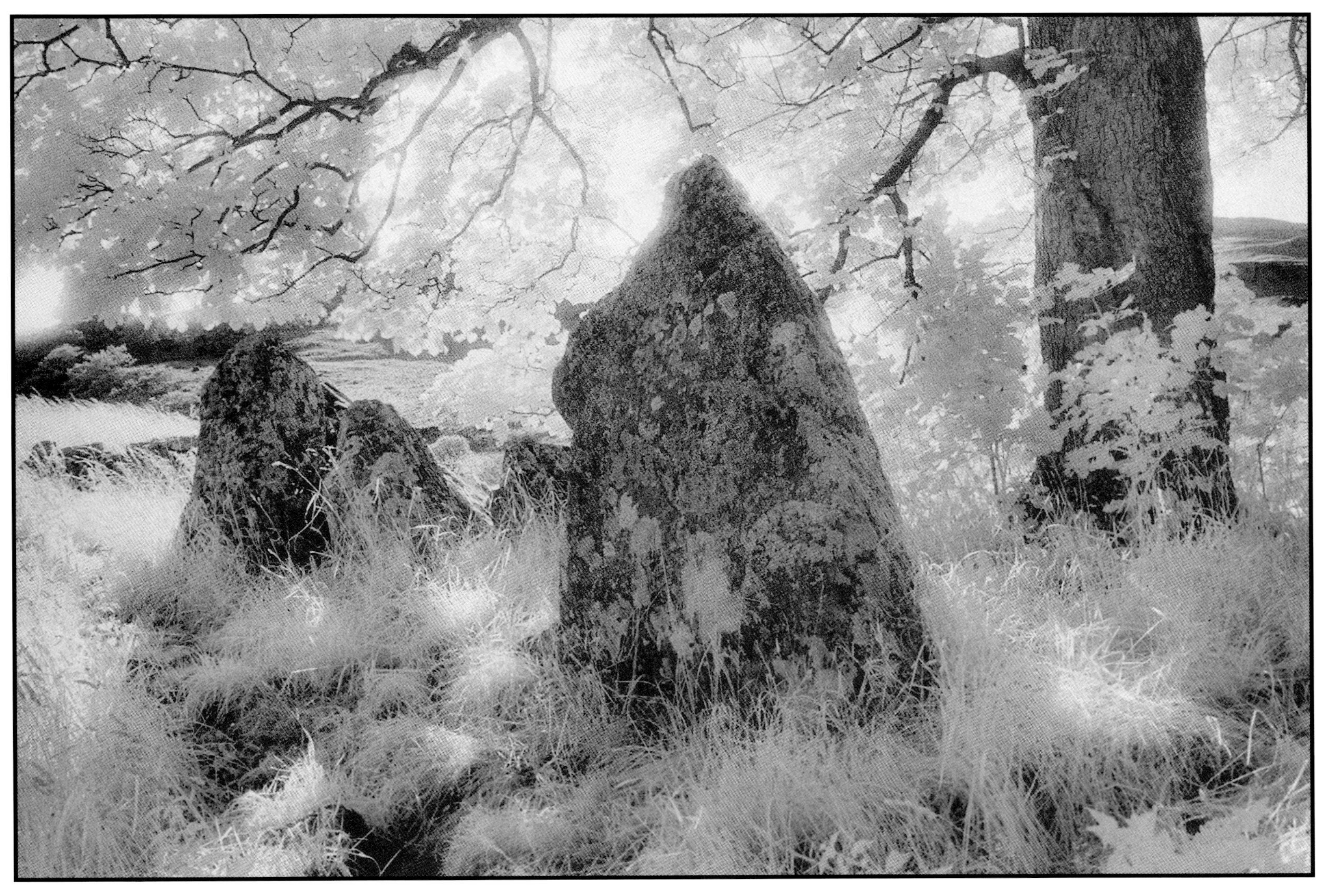

(top left)
Breeze

(bottom left)
Firmly rooted

(above)
Ardnamurchan

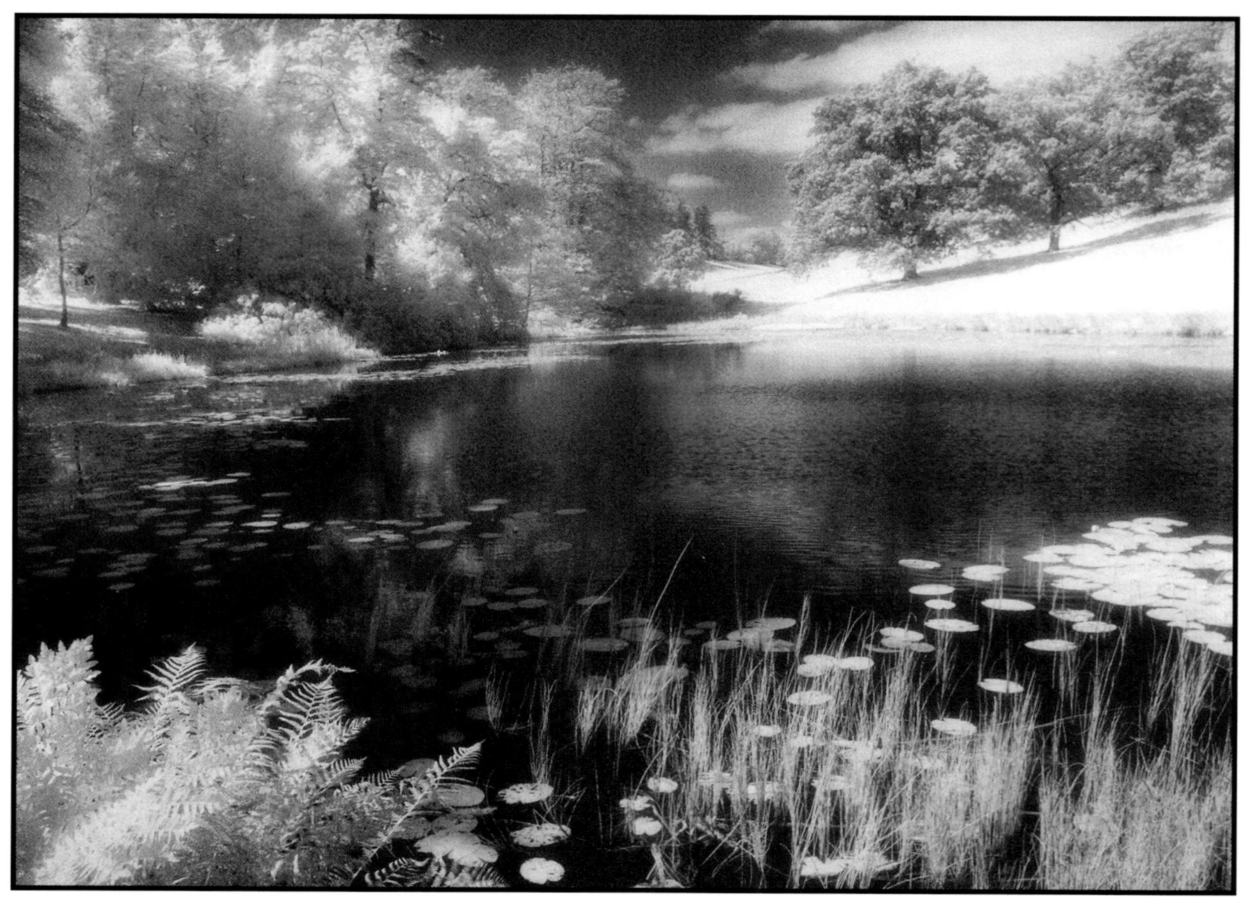

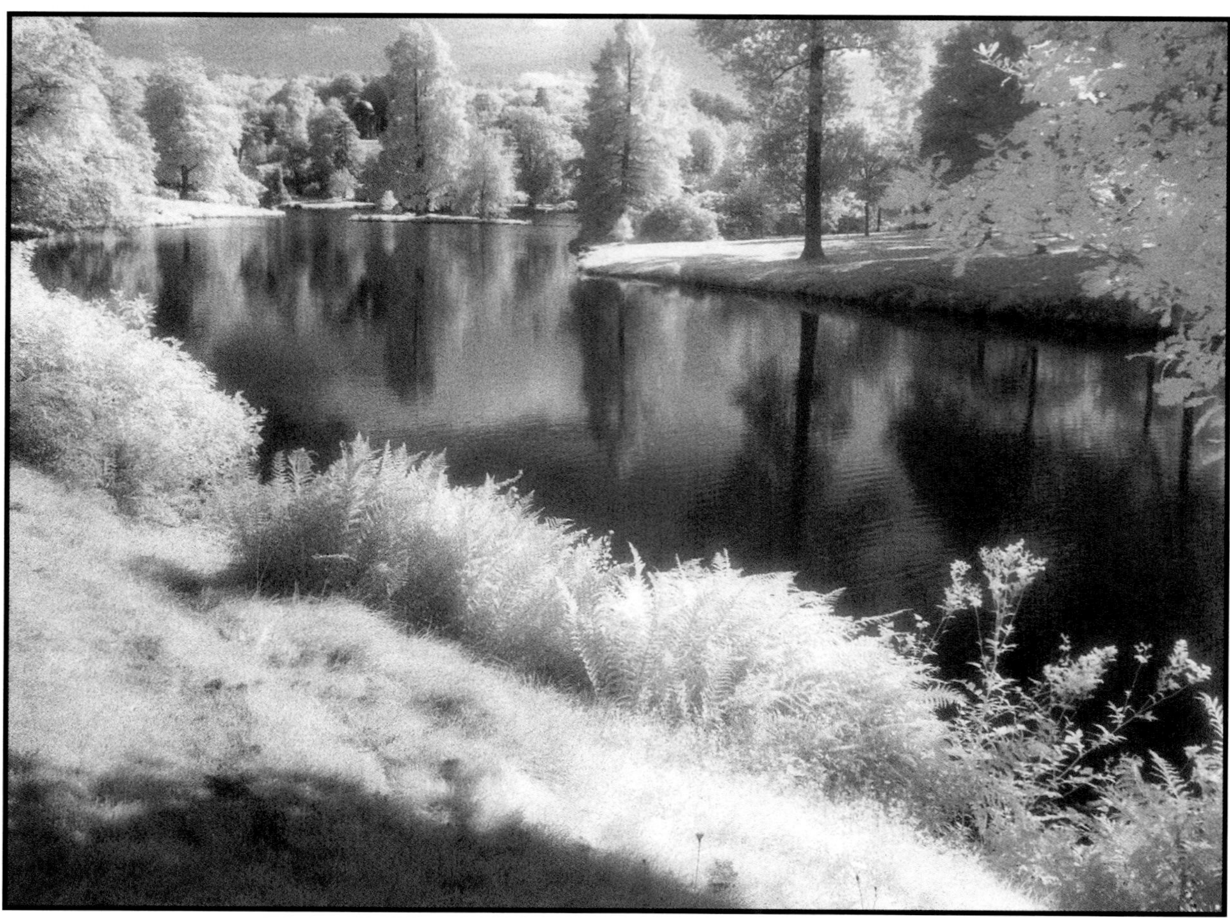

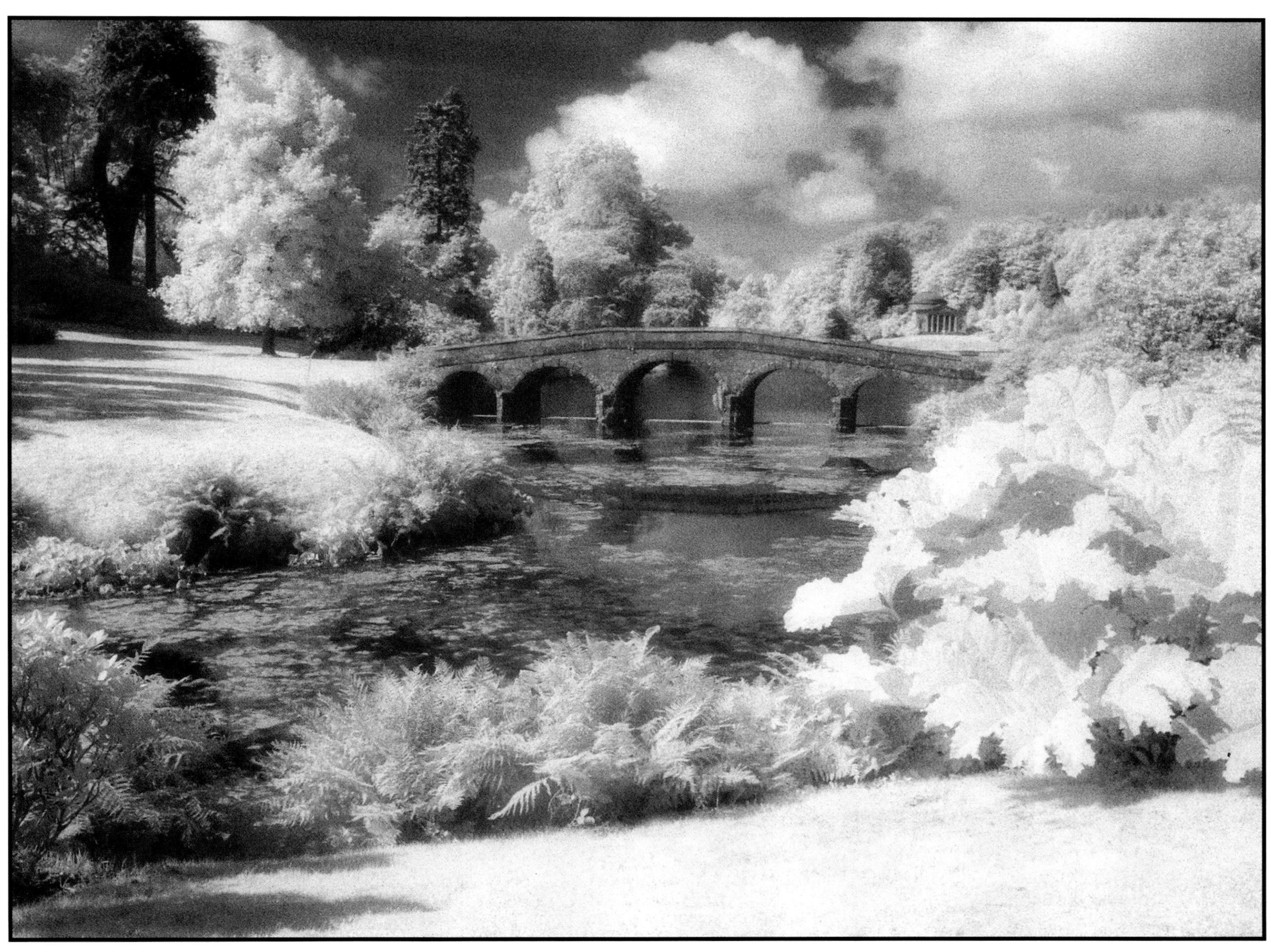

(top left)
Lily pond

(bottom left)
Stourhead II

(above)
Stourhead

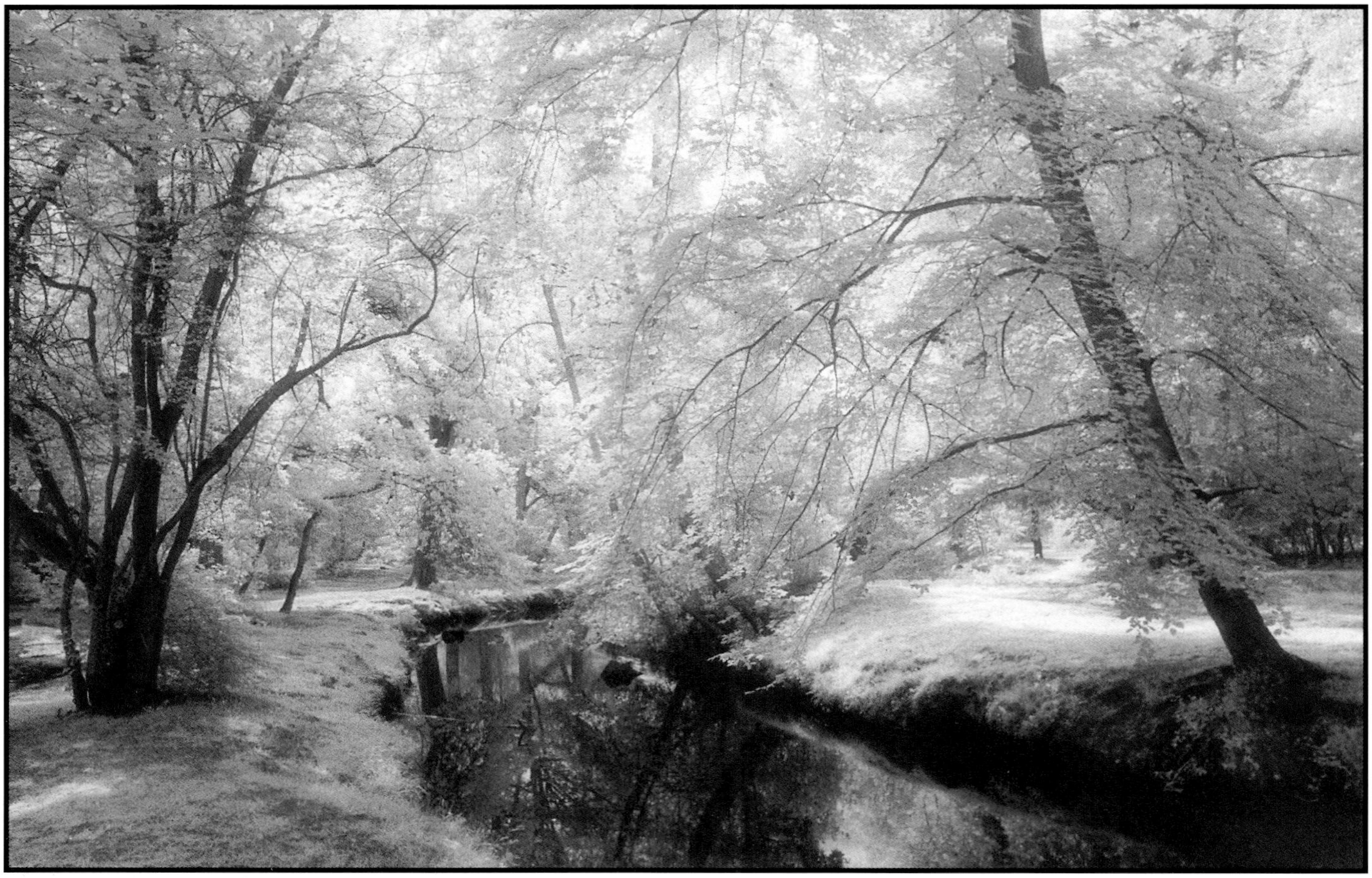

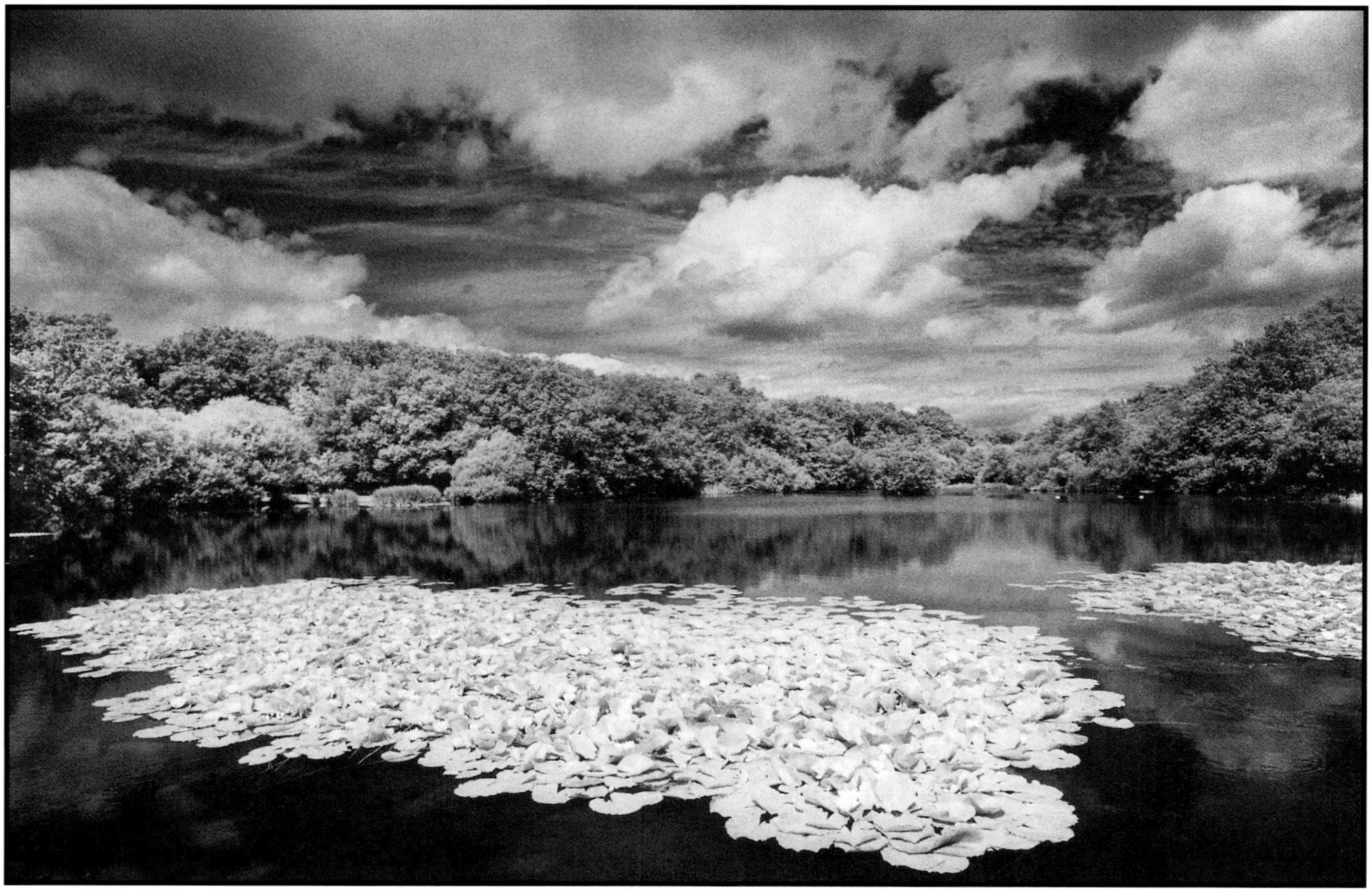

(top left)
Ipley

(bottom left)
Waterlilies

(right)
Follow the light

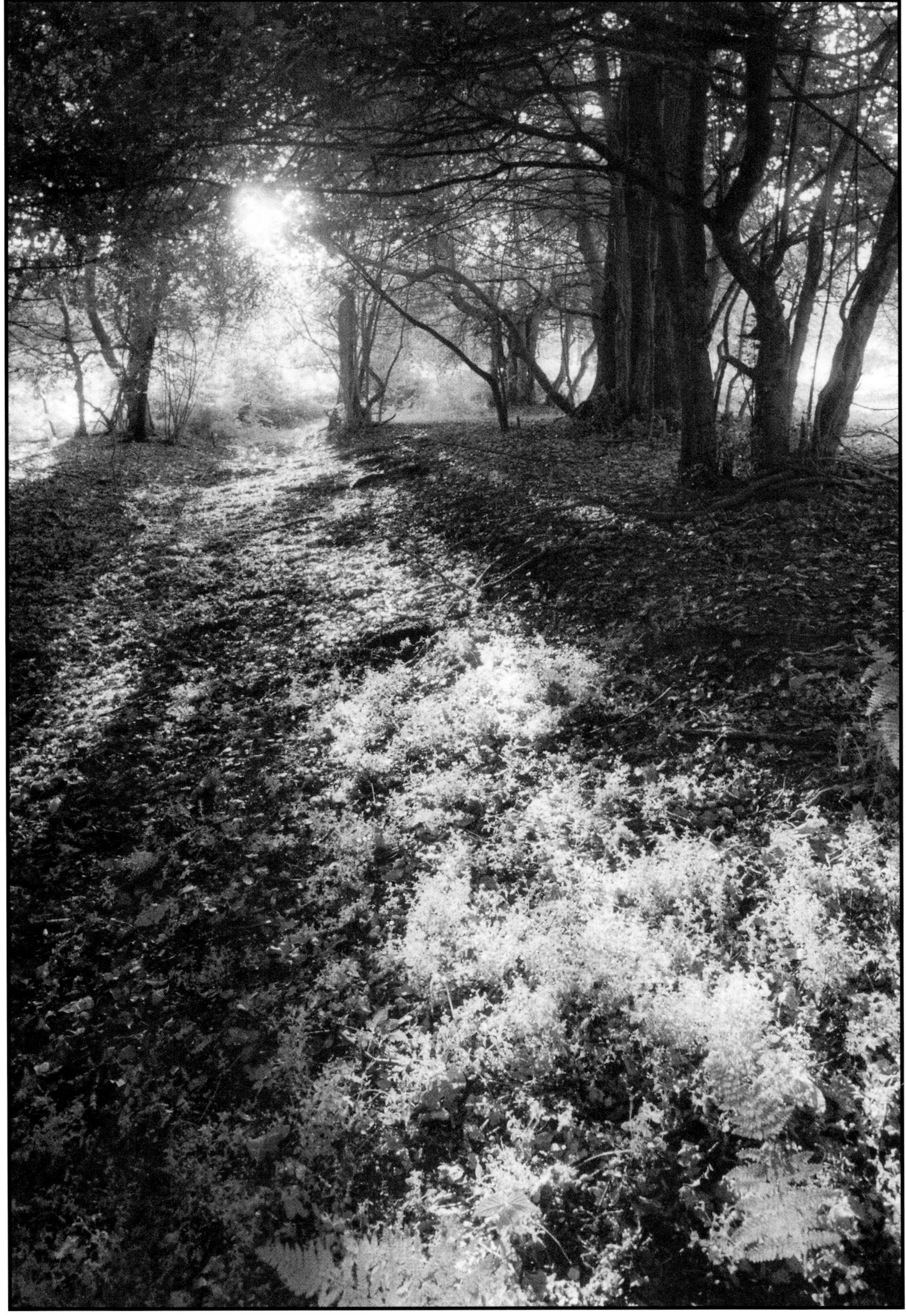

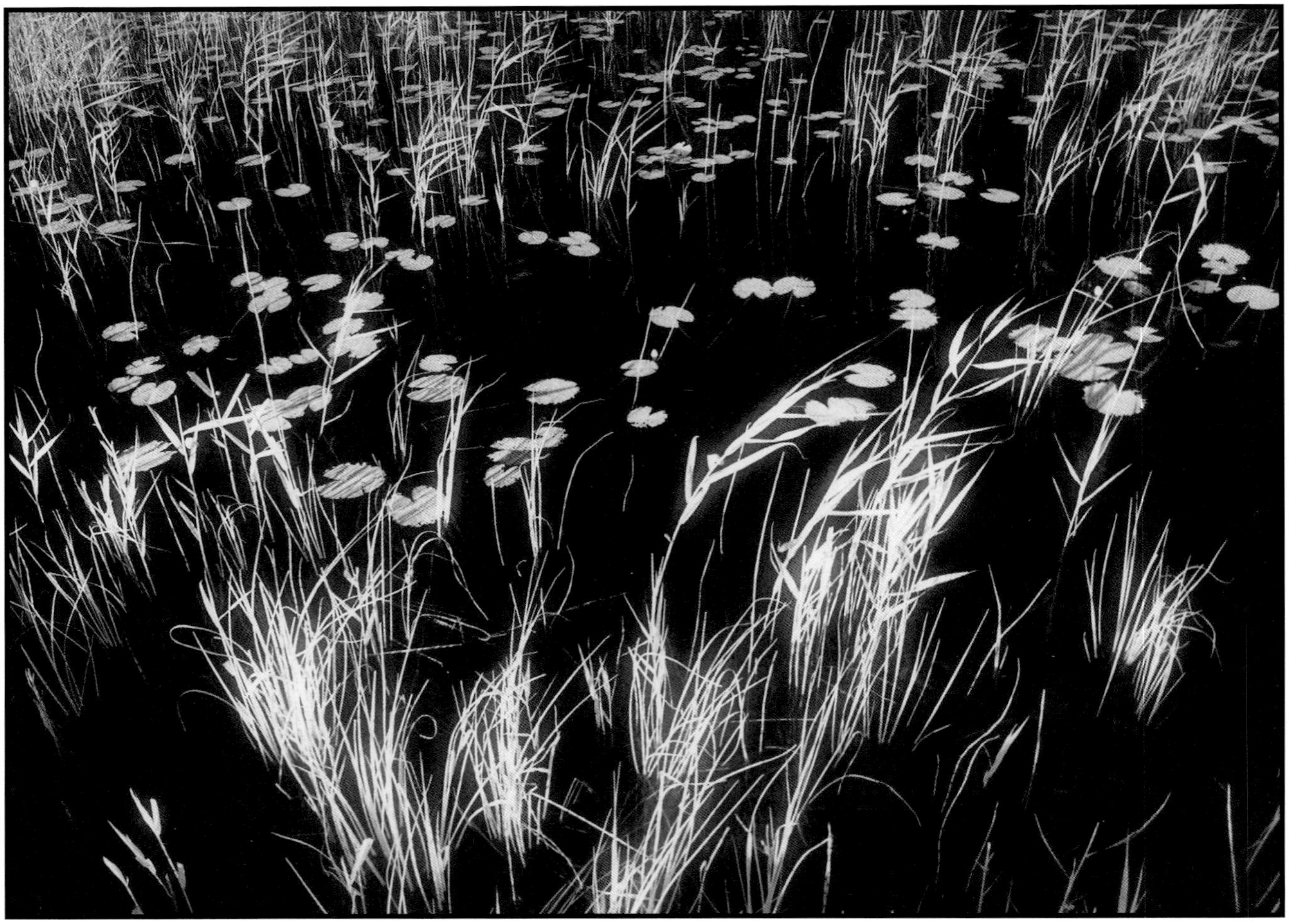

Lilies

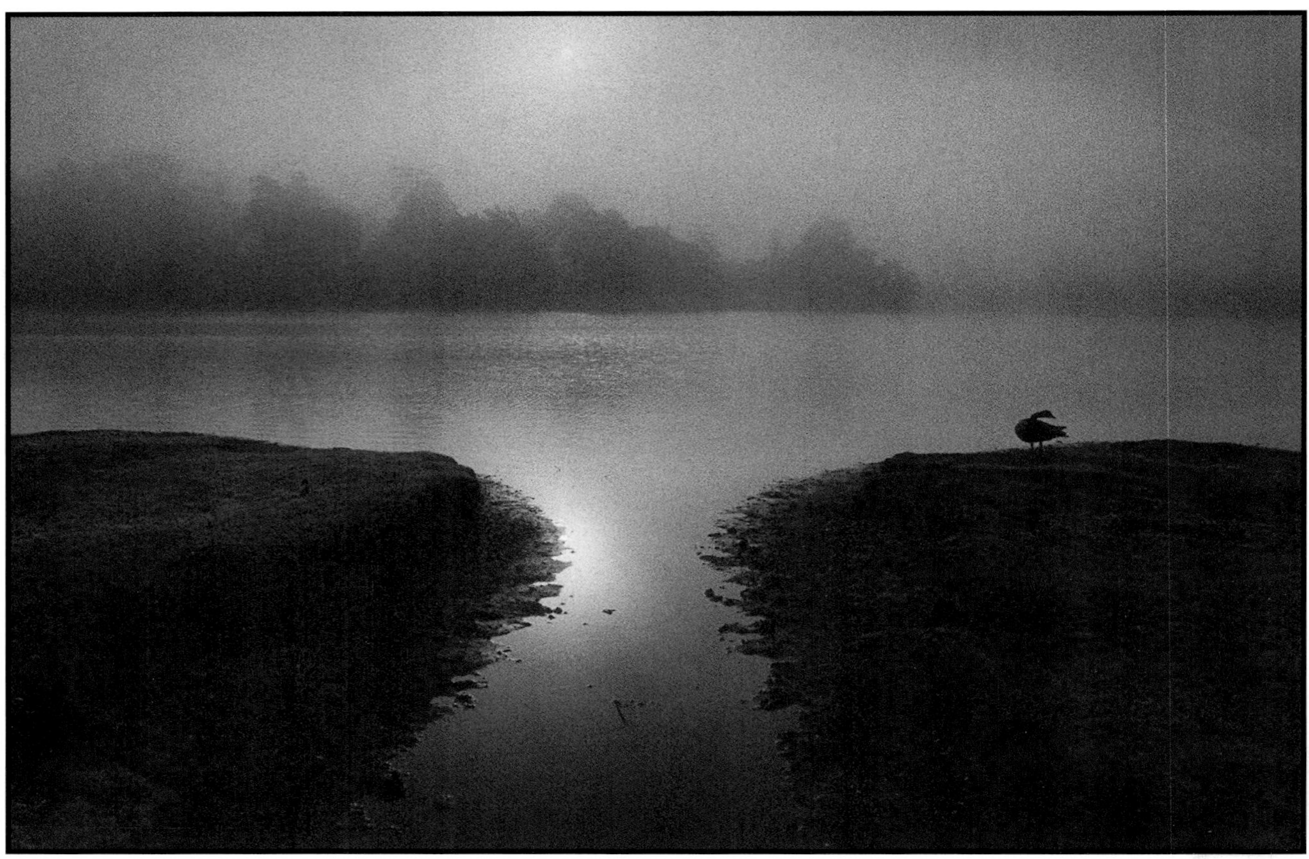

Dawn at Beaulieu Pond